Microbiology and Biotechnology

Pauline Lowrie and Susan Wells

Series editor
Fred Webber

CAMBRIDGE
UNIVERSITY PRESS

Published by the Press Syndicate of the University of Cambridge
The Pitt Building, Trumpington Street, Cambridge CB2 1RP
40 West 20th Street, New York, NY 10011-4211, USA
10 Stamford Road, Oakleigh, Melbourne 3166, Australia

© University of Cambridge Local Examinations Syndicate 1994

First published 1994
Reprinted 1996

Printed in Great Britain at the University Press, Cambridge

A catalogue record for this book is available from the British Library

ISBN 0 521 42204 3 paperback

Designed and produced by Gecko Ltd, Bicester, Oxon

This book is one of a series produced to support individual modules within the Cambridge Modular Sciences scheme. Teachers should note that written examinations will be set on the content of each module as defined in the syllabus. This book is the authors' interpretation of the module.

Acknowledgements

Many thanks to Sue Kearsey for her meticulous and thoughtful editing which the authors greatly appreciate. However, the authors accept full responsibility for the final content of the book.

The authors would also like to thank June Withenshaw for her help with the simulated newspaper on page 48.

The publishers would like to thank Michael Reiss and Stephen Shaw for their invaluable help with the text.

Photographs

1.1a, 1.21, NIBSC/Science Photo Library; 1.1b, Barry Dowsett/Science Photo Library; 1.1c, CNRI/Science Photo Library; 1.6, Dr L Caro/Science Photo Library; 1.17a, Manfred Kage/Science Photo Library; 1.17b, 1.24, Biophoto Associates; 1.17c Dr Jeremy Burgess/Science Photo Library; 1.17d David Scharff/Science Photo Library; 2.1 Peter Gould; 3.1, Ronald Sheridan/Ancient Art and Architecture Collection; 4.1, James Holmes/Celltech Ltd/Science Photo Library; 4.2, Philippe Plailly/Science Photo Library; 4.4, Geoff Tompkinson/Science Photo Library; 5.1a, b, courtesy of Zeneca BioProducts; 5.5, courtesy of Wearne Associates; 5.7a, b, courtesy of Gist-brocades; 6.1, courtesy of DISTA Products Ltd; 7.4a, b, courtesy of Novo Nordisk; 7.5, Sean Sprague/Panos Pictures.

Cover: A coloured TEM of *Salmonella enteritidis*. The outer membrane, cell contents and hair-like flagellae can be seen.
(Alfred Pasieka/Science Photo Library)

Contents

Chapter one

Microbiology

By the end of this chapter you should be able to:

1 describe the major characteristics of the four groups of microorganisms, the Prokaryotae (Bacteria and Cyanobacteria), Protoctista, Fungi and Viruses;

2 describe, as a result of your observations, the structures and asexual reproduction of a named bacterium;

3 describe the general structure and life cycle of viruses, including a named bacteriophage and a named retrovirus.

The main purpose of this book is to give you an understanding of some of the many ways in which microbiology and biotechnology affect our lives. It is also important that you should understand why microorganisms are particularly suitable for use in industrial processes. However, before you can properly understand all these things, it is necessary that you learn a little about the structure and function of the different kinds of microorganisms.

Microorganisms (microbes) are so small that they can only be seen individually with a good quality light microscope. **Microbiology** is the study of microorganisms and can be sub-divided into several specialist branches such as **bacteriology** (the study of bacteria), **mycology** (the study of fungi) and **virology** (the study of viruses). There are four major groups of microorganisms: Prokaryotae, Protoctista, Fungi and Viruses.

All prokaryotic organisms are grouped into the kingdom Prokaryotae. Prokaryotic cells do not have a true, membrane-bound nucleus and organelles, nor flagella with the typical 9 + 2 arrangement of microtubules such as are found in the eukaryotes (see *Foundation Biology* in this series). The kingdom Fungi and the kingdom Protoctista are both eukaryotic. Viruses do not fit into a classification of living organisms because they are dependent on other cells for their reproduction.

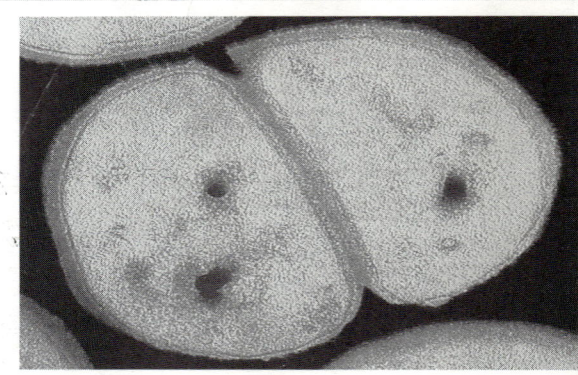

● **Figure 1.1** Some examples of bacteria.

a Scanning electron micrograph (SEM) of the rod-shaped Gram negative bacterium *Escherichia coli* (× 14 500).

b TEM of *Campylobacter jejunii* which causes food poisoning in humans. The bacterium moves by means of two single terminal flagella (× 9000).

c Transmission EM of *Staphylococcus aureus*. The cell is in the process of cell division with the new cell wall half completed across the centre of the individual (× 62 000).

Structure	Features
*cell wall	10–100 nm thick, net-like, multilayered structure made of murein (a polymer of polysaccharide and peptide components); two distinct types are distinguished by the Gram's stain: **Gram positive**; thicker, rigid murein network filled with peptides and polysaccharides, e.g. *Lactobacillus* **Gram negative**: thinner, more complex, made of murein coated with a smooth layer of lipids, e.g. *Escherichia coli*
*cell surface membrane	phospholipid bilayer with proteins floating in membrane; proteins include enzymes involved in respiration*, photosynthesis•, nucleic acid synthesis* and electron transport*
*ribosomes	small 70S ribosomes are the site of protein synthesis
*cytoplasm	uniform with few organelles; contains storage granules, ribosomes, plasmids; a nucleoid (nuclear region) is usually present
•flagellum	used in the locomotion of many motile bacteria; a rigid, hollow cylinder of protein, the base of which rotates propelling the cell along, e.g. *Rhizobium* and *Azotobacter*
•capsule (slime layer)	an outer protective layer visible with negative (background) staining; it protects against chemicals and desiccation, stores waste products and protects the bacterium from attack by phagocytic cells; it helps bacteria to form colonies and is important in soil bacteria where it helps bind soil particles into crumbs, e.g. *Azotobacter*
•photosynthetic membranes	sac-like or tubular infoldings of the cell surface membrane provide a large surface area for the inclusion of bacteriochlorophyll and other photosynthetic pigments in photoautotrophic bacteria, e.g. *Chromatium*
•mesosomes	tightly folded infoldings of the cell surface membrane, thought to be the site of respiration; also involved in cell division and the uptake of DNA
•pili (fimbriae)	numerous projections from the cell surface membrane through the cell wall found all over some bacterial cells; they are used in conjugation to bind cells together and exchange genetic material; they also have an antigenic effect, e.g. *Salmonella*
•endospores	a hard outer covering forms a resistant endospore which ensures survival in severe conditions of drought, toxic chemicals and extremes of temperature, e.g. *Bacillus anthracis* spores, which cause the disease anthrax, are known to be viable after 50 years in the soil

● **Table 1.1** Summary of the structure of bacteria (* always present, • sometimes present)

Kingdom Prokaryotae

This kingdom contains all the prokaryotic organisms, that is the Bacteria and Cyanobacteria (the blue-green bacteria, formerly called blue-green algae).

Bacteria

Examples: *Escherichia coli, Streptococcus lactis, Bacillus subtilis, Staphylococcus aureus*

Bacteria are found in a wide range of habitats: in soil, air, water, as well as in or on the surface of animals and plants. They range in size from 0.1–10 µm in length and are usually found in enormous numbers: one gram of soil may contain 100 million bacteria. Some bacteria have an optimum temperature for growth which is greater than 45 °C and are called thermophilic bacteria; some can even thrive in hot volcanic springs at around 70 °C. Psychrophilic bacteria, on the other hand, grow best at temperatures below 20 °C and can withstand long periods of freezing. Bacteria are important because they help to decay and recycle organic waste. Some cause disease, but most are harmless and many are of increasing economic importance in biotechnology.

Structure of bacteria

Figure 1.1 shows a variety of shapes of bacteria and *figure 1.2* shows the structure of a generalised bacterial cell. *Table 1.1* gives more detail of their structure.

1 μm

cell wall*
mesosome
DNA*
pili
70S ribosome*
photosynthetic membranes
food reserve granule*
flagellum
cell surface membrane*
capsule or slime layer
cytoplasm*

*structures always present in bacteria

● **Figure 1.2** A generalised rod-shaped bacterial cell.

The bacterial cell wall

In 1884 Christian Gram developed a way of staining bacteria which divided them into two groups. These were called Gram positive and Gram negative. It is now known that bacteria have two different types of cell wall which the staining technique reveals.

✳ The technique developed by Gram is still commonly used today. It involves heat-fixing a smear of bacteria to a clean microscope slide and then flooding it with crystal violet. All bacteria take up this stain. The smear is washed with Gram's iodine to fix the stain and then decolourised with alcohol or propanone. Gram positive bacteria retain the crystal violet/iodine complex to colour purple, but Gram negative bacteria do not. Finally the smear is counter-stained with a red stain such as safranin or carbol fuchsin. Gram negative bacteria take up this stain and become red. Gram positive bacteria stay purple.

The different reaction to the stain is due to the structure of the two basic types of cell wall *(figure 1.3)*. Gram positive bacteria have a cell surface membrane surrounded by a rigid cell wall about 20–80 nm thick. This rigid layer is made of the peptidoglycan **murein**, which has a complex three-dimensional structure. Gram negative bacteria also have a rigid layer outside the surface membrane but it is much thinner, only 2–3 nm thick. On the outside of this is an outer membrane which contains lipopolysaccharides instead of phospho-lipids. This forms an extra physical barrier to substances, such as antibiotics and enzymes like lysozyme, which normally destroy or inhibit bacteria. The crystal violet/iodine complex is a large molecule and it is thought that, during Gram staining, it becomes trapped inside the cell wall, whereas it is more easily washed out of the thinner Gram negative cell wall.

capsule or slime layer (may be absent)

peptidoglycan (murein) wall

10 nm

antigen on outer surface
lipopolysaccharide
outer membrane
peptidoglycan (murein) layer
cell surface membrane
cytosol

Gram positive cell wall

Gram negative cell wall

● **Figure 1.3** The structure of bacterial cell walls based on electron micrographs of the cell walls of *Bacillus* (Gram positive) and *E. coli* (Gram negative).

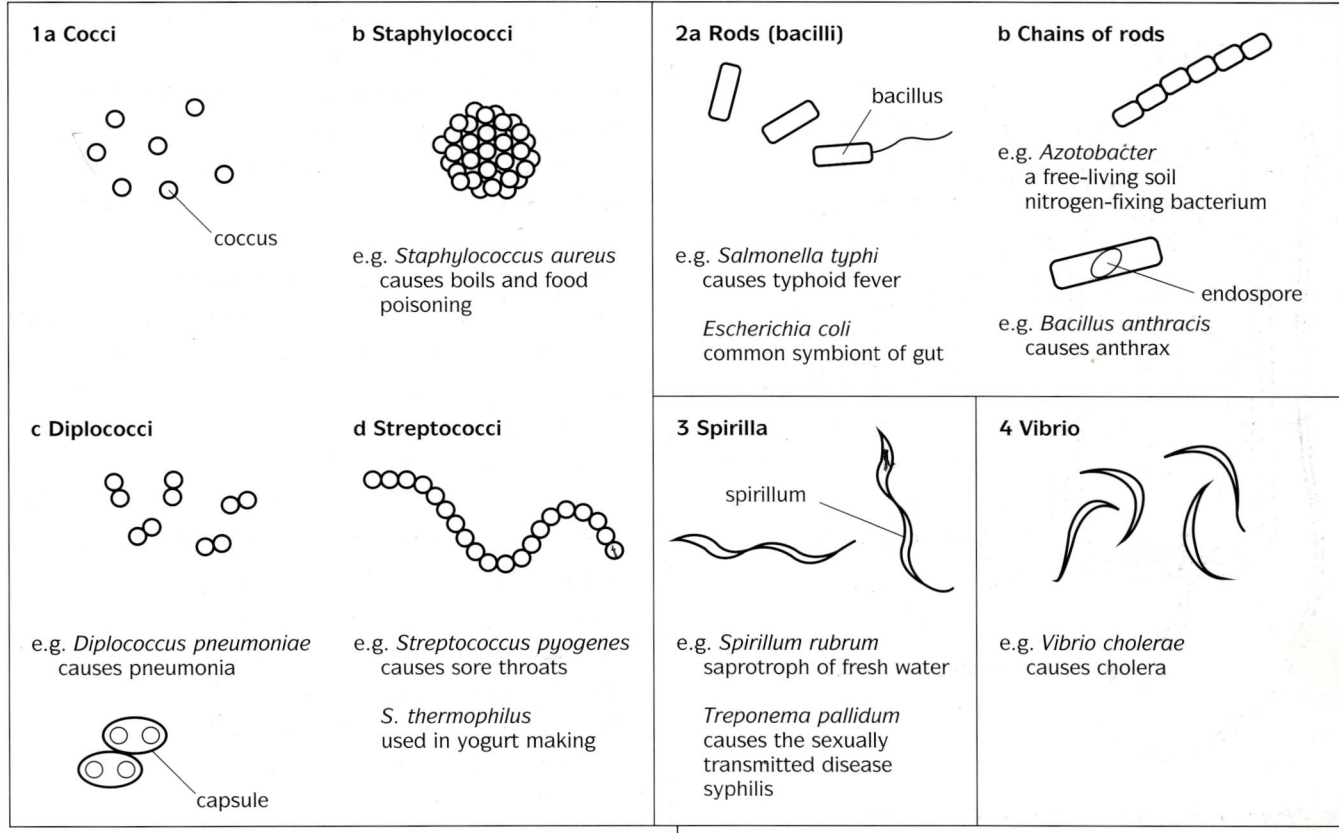

● **Figure 1.4** The forms (shapes) of bacteria.

Shapes of bacteria

When viewed with a microscope, bacteria show several distinct shapes and these may be used to help in identification *(figure 1.4)*.

Reproduction

Bacteria grow very quickly in favourable conditions. The generation time may be as little as 20 minutes, though for many species it is 15–20 hours. Division is usually by binary fission *(figure 1.5)*.

✳ Binary fission in *Escherichia coli*

1 The circular bacterial chromosome divides but there is no mitotic spindle. The chromosome attaches itself to the cell membrane or, in some cases, to the mesosome.
2 A septum starts to be synthesised to divide the cell. This often starts growing where there are mesosomes.
3 The septum grows right across the cell, dividing it into two daughter cells.

● **Figure 1.5** Binary fission in bacteria.

Conjugation, transformation and transduction

Some bacteria have 'mating' cells which come together and are joined by their pili in a process known as **conjugation** *(figure 1.6)*. The donor passes a plasmid called the F factor, or fertility factor, to the recipient. The **plasmid** is a small, circular, non-chromosomal piece of DNA. Genetic information on the F factor provides the bacterial cell with everything needed to be a donor, including the capacity to synthesise the sex pilus. The F factor may exist as a free element within the cytoplasm, replicating independently of the bacterial chromosome, or it may become incorporated within the bacterial chromosome and be replicated whenever the chromosome replicates.

Transformation occurs when one bacterium releases DNA which is absorbed by a second bacterium. The second cell therefore acquires new characteristics.

Transduction is where new genes are inserted into the chromosome of a bacterium by a bacterio-phage virus (see page 21).

● *Figure 1.6* Conjugation in *E. coli*.

Conjugation, transformation and transduction are not forms of sexual reproduction since fertilisation does not occur. In each of the above cases, DNA has been transferred from a donor to a recipient.

Plasmids

The cytoplasm of certain bacteria contains small circles of DNA called plasmids which are able to replicate independently of the main circular chromosome. Plasmids are known to carry genes which may help the bacterium to survive in adverse conditions. For example, plasmids known as R-factors cause resistance to antibiotics, virus infection and ultraviolet radiation. Plasmids can be transferred to another bacterium in conjugation, transformation or transduction.

The economic importance of bacteria

Some genera of bacteria contain species which are commercially useful and some which are harmful to humans. For example, most *Bacillus* spp. live in the soil, and are either aerobes or facultative anaerobes. *Bacillus subtilis* is a strict aerobe which is used in industry as a source of enzymes such as amylases. *Bacillus thuringiensis* has become important in genetic engineering because it causes a paralytic disease in many caterpillars and has been used to produce insect-resistant plants (page 61). However, some species of *Bacillus* are pathogenic, such as *Bacillus anthracis* which causes the disease anthrax.

Table 1.2 lists some bacteria which are commercially useful. Some of these are described in more detail in later chapters. Other bacteria are useful in different ways, for example in recycling nutrients and fixing nitrogen in ecological cycles. *Rhizobium* is a nitrogen-fixing bacterium which is present in the soil. It invades the root hairs of leguminous plants, causing the cells to divide and form nitrogen-fixing nodules. Many species of *Clostridium* can also fix nitrogen, such as *C. welchii*, *C. pastorianum* and *C. butyricum*, and are important in the nitrogen cycle.

Table 1.3 lists some bacteria which cause disease in humans. Some belong to genera which contain

Name	Gram stain	Form (shape)	Use
Lactobacillus bulgaricus	+ve	rods	yogurt
Streptomyces thermophilus	+ve	filamentous	yogurt
Streptococcus lactus	+ve	cocci	cheese
Streptococcus cremoris	+ve	cocci	cheese
Methylophilus methylotropus	variable	cocci	methane, methanol
Clostridium acetobutylicum	+ve	rods	propanone (acetone) and butanol
Leuconostoc mesenteroides	+ve	cocci	dextran
*Bacillus subtilis**	+ve	rods	enzymes
Streptomyces spp.	+ve	filamentous	antibiotics
*Escherichia coli**	−ve	rods	insulin, growth hormone, interferon
Pseudomonas denitrificans	−ve	rods	vitamin B_{12}

* using genetic engineering

● **Table 1.2** Some useful bacteria

Name	Gram stain	Form (shape)	Disease
Staphylococcus aureus	+ve	cocci	boils
Salmonella typhimurium	−ve	rods	food poisoning
Salmonella typhi	−ve	rods	typhoid fever
Mycobacterium tuberculosis	variable	fine rods	tuberculosis
Bordetella pertussis	−ve	very short rods	whooping cough
Neisseria gonorrhoea	−ve	cocci	gonorrhoea
Treponema pallidum	variable	long spirals	syphilis
Vibrio cholerae	−ve	curved rods	cholera
Clostridium tetani	+ve	rods	tetanus
Clostridium botulinum	+ve	rods	botulism
Corynebacterium diptheriae	+ve	short rods	diptheria
Listeria spp.	+ve	round-ended rods	listeriosis
Shigella sonnei	−ve	rods	dysentery
Yersinia pestis	−ve	small rods	plague

● **Table 1.3** Some harmful bacteria

many non-pathogenic species, for example most species of *Staphylococcus* are facultative anaerobes which are found in the normal microflora of the skin. *S. aureus* normally causes boils. However, one strain of this species has developed resistance to most antibiotics, through overuse of antibiotics in treating patients, and has become a major problem in hospitals in many countries.

SAQ 1.1

Match the words on the left to the definitions on the right.

plasmid	slimy layer surrounding some bacterial cell walls
mesosome	circular piece of DNA not joined to chromosome
cell wall	made of pilin, used in conjugation in some species
capsule	the main component of this is the peptidoglycan murein
pilus	infolding of membrane, probably used in cell division

Cyanobacteria (blue-green bacteria)

Examples: *Anabaena cylindris, Nostoc muscorum, Spirulina platensis*

Cyanobacteria are prokaryotic microorganisms similar to the true bacteria. They are photosynthetic but are not true algae because they do not have membrane-bound nuclei, and are considered to be very ancient life-forms. They have been found in fossil remains from over three billion years ago and may have been some of the first living organisms to evolve on Earth. They are found in the surface layer of fresh and sea water. On land they will grow wherever there is both light and moisture and are found as slime on the surface of mud, rocks, wood and on some living organisms. Their name comes from the photosynthetic pigments which give them a distinct dark greenish-blue colour.

Structure of cyanobacteria

Blue-greens have a typical prokaryotic cell structure since they have a naked coil of DNA and no true nucleus (*figure 1.7*). The cell wall is similar in structure and composition to that of

● **Figure 1.7** Diagram of a typical blue-green cell (based on electron micrographs).

Labels:
- gelatinous sheath (slime layer)
- cell wall (similar to Gram negative bacteria)
- cell surface membrane
- cytoplasm
- nuclear zone with DNA
- photosynthetic lamellae
- gas vacuole
- phycobilisome (contains photosynthetic pigments)
- 70S ribosomes
- 2 μm

Gram negative bacteria. Protein synthesis takes place on 70S ribosomes in the cytoplasm. Blue-greens are photosynthetic. They have chlorophyll and carotenoid pigments incorporated into infoldings of the cell surface membrane, called **lamellae**. They also have photosynthetic pigments, such as phycocyanin and phycoerythrin, which are present in phycobilisomes. These give the cells their distinctive colouration. The cells may occur singly or in colonies, but members of a colony remain independent.

Nitrogen fixation

Only a very few organisms are capable of fixing atmospheric nitrogen by reducing it to ammonia and combining it with organic acids to produce amino acids and proteins. Nitrogen-fixing bacteria can do this and so can some blue-greens. Cells able to fix nitrogen contain the enzyme nitrogenase. This enzyme is inactivated by oxygen and so conditions inside the nitrogen-fixing cell have to be anaerobic. Some blue-greens, such as *Anabaena*, have special thick-walled cells called **heterocysts**. *Anabaena* has filaments made up of many normal photosynthetic cells that produce sugars and oxygen. Scattered along the filaments are a few distinct heterocyst cells that are able to fix atmospheric nitrogen in this way *(figure 1.8)*.

Many filamentous blue-greens are also able to produce **akinetes**, or spores. These are able to survive adverse conditions, such as a period of over-population known as an algal 'bloom', and seem to develop from a vegetative cell near to a heterocyst. The cell increases in size and accumulates large food reserves. Photosynthesis within the akinete is reduced and gas vacuoles disappear. This means that the akinete slowly sinks to the bottom of the water. It may survive for several years, and will germinate as soon as conditions become favourable.

The economic importance of blue-greens

Spirulina platensis is a filamentous blue-green found naturally in shallow alkaline lakes in parts of Africa and South America. For thousands of years it has been collected and dried by the local people and used as a food. It is often fried or put in soups and sauces; it is also used as cattle food. *Nostoc* is another blue-green which is used as a food in Peru and in South-East Asia.

In agriculture, nitrogen-fixing blue-greens may be used as organic fertilisers. They are grown on a large scale in China, India and the Philippines, particularly where rice is cultivated in paddy fields. The water may be seeded with a starter culture of blue-greens at the beginning of the growing season. This method has been shown to increase the yield of rice by 15–20%.

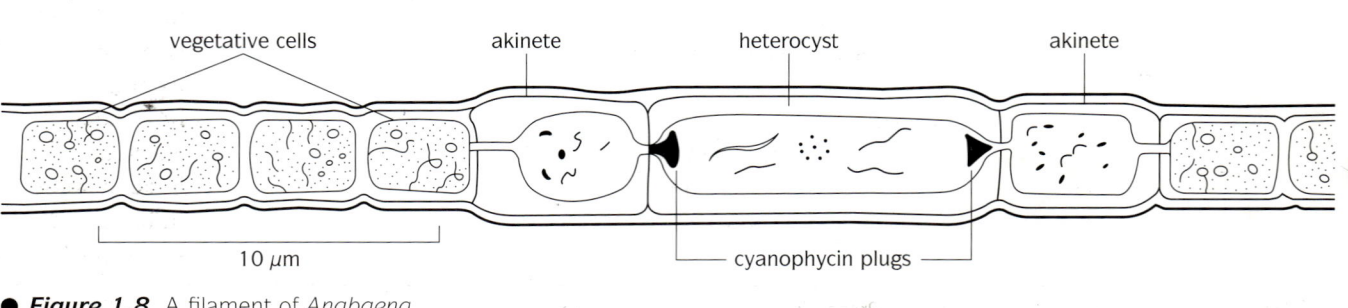

Labels: vegetative cells, akinete, heterocyst, akinete, 10 μm, cyanophycin plugs

● **Figure 1.8** A filament of *Anabaena*.

Research is taking place into the use of blue-greens in a solar energy conversion system. *Anabaena cylindrica* has heterocysts and is able to give off oxygen by photosynthesis in the vegetative cells. In the absence of nitrogen it gives off hydrogen by nitrogenase-catalysed electron transfer to H^+ ions in the heterocysts. Both oxygen and hydrogen are in demand industrially.

SAQ 1.2

Why are blue-greens classified as prokaryotes?

Phylum	Example	Structure	Locomotion	Nutrition	Reproduction	Importance
Rhizopoda	*Amoeba proteus*	0.5 mm long, single cell, cytoplasm exists in two states: plasmasol and plasmagel	pseudopodia	phagocytosis and food vacuoles formed	asexual by binary fission	*Entamoeba histolytica* causes amoebic dysentery
Apicomplexa (sporozoans)	*Plasmodium vivax*	10 µm long, different forms during life cycle: sporozoites long and thin, infective particles; merozoites smaller, pear-shaped	microtubules which slide over each other to penetrate host tissue	phagocytosis	asexual by multiple fission and sexual by gametocytes	*P. vivax* causes parasitic disease malaria, mosquito is the vector
Ciliophora (ciliates)	*Paramecium caudatum*	100 µm long, enclosed by a pellicle with cilia, oral groove leads to 'mouth' with cytostome	cilia beat together in coordinated way	cilia beat and sweep food towards cytostome, where phagocytosis takes place	asexual by binary fission, sexual by conjugation	live in fresh water, important in sewage treatment and decomposition
Zoomastigina (flagellates)	*Trypanosoma gambiense*	unicellular, elongated spindle-shaped, contains trophonucleus (also concerned with nutrition) and kinetoplast near posterior end to control movement	single flagellum bound to the trypanosome along the length of the cell by the undulating membrane, free beyond that; wave-like movements propel the cell through the viscous blood plasma	heterotrophic, parasitic; lives in human blood plasma; soluble nutrients diffuse into cell	longitudinal binary fission in the blood of the host starting at anterior end	causes trypanosomiasis or 'sleeping sickness'; spread by the tsetse fly as it feeds on human blood; symptoms include headache, anaemia, inflammation of brain and spinal cord

● *Table 1.4* A summary of the Kingdom Protoctista (continued on page 12)

Phylum	Example	Structure	Locomotion	Nutrition	Reproduction	Importance
Euglenophyta (euglenoid flagellates)	*Euglena viridis*	300 μm long slender cell, pellicle covers outside, blunt anterior end with reservoir	two flagella arise from base of reservoir, light-sensitive stigma used to orientate movement	chloroplasts present, therefore photoauto-trophic; stores food granules of paramylum, needs vitamins B_1 and B_{12} for growth	longitudinal binary fission (asexual)	found in fresh and salt water, and damp soil
Chlorophyta (green algae)	*Chlorella vulgaris*	50 μm diameter, unicellular green alga, thin cellulose cell wall, large cup-shaped chloroplast	floats in water	photoauto-trophic	asexual by fission (*figure 1.9*)	freshwater ponds
Oomycota (oomycetes)	*Phytophthora infestans* or *Pythium* spp.	long thread-like hyphae, aseptate (no cross walls), cytoplasm contains many nuclei, cell wall of chitin with mannan and glucan polymers	spore stages have two flagella	heterotrophic (plant parasites), hyphae secrete enzymes, food digested extra-cellularly, soluble nutrients absorbed	asexual by motile spores formed inside a sporangium on a special hypha (sporangiophore); sexual by fusion of male antheridium and female oogonium to produce sexual oospore which survives adverse conditions	*Phytophthora* causes late blight of potatoes (as in Irish potato famine) *Pythium* causes damping-off in seedlings

● **Table 1.4** (cont.)

SAQ 1.3

It is thought that blue-greens may have been the first photosynthetic organisms on Earth and that they represent a very early stage in the evolution of life. Give as many reasons as you can why this might be so.

Kingdom Protoctista

This kingdom has been created to contain all groups of eukaryotic organisms which are neither animals, plants, fungi nor prokaryotes. These groups are not really related though they do have some similarities. They include all protozoa, all nucleated algae and the slime moulds (*table 1.4* and *figure 1.9*).

The protozoa is a collective term for the phyla Rhizopoda, Zoomastigina, Apicomplexa and Ciliophora. They are found wherever moisture is present, in sea water, fresh water and soil. There are commensal, symbiotic and parasitic species in addition to many free-living types. Protozoa are eukaryotic. The nucleus has a nuclear envelope,

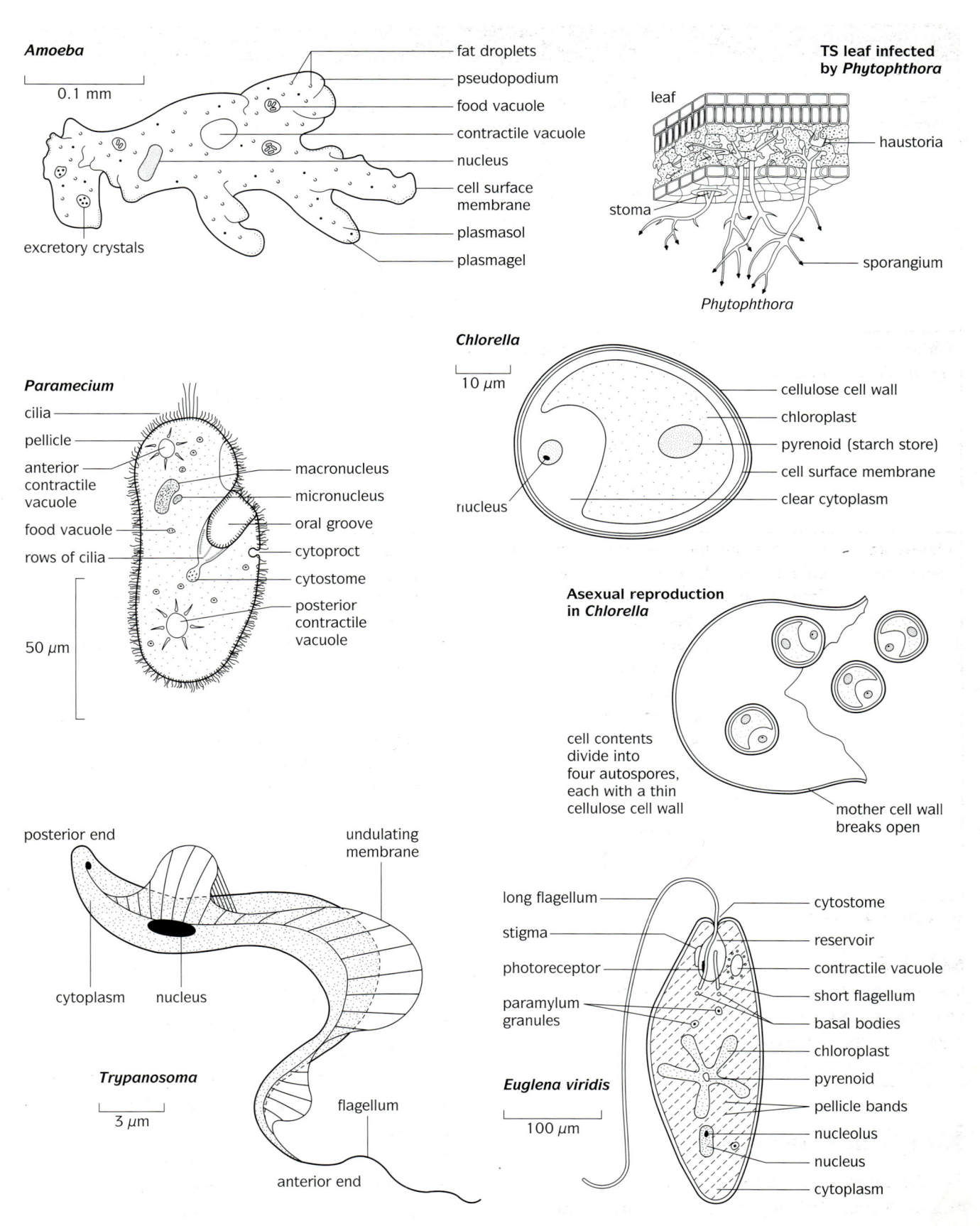

Amoeba

0.1 mm

- fat droplets
- pseudopodium
- food vacuole
- contractile vacuole
- nucleus
- cell surface membrane
- plasmasol
- plasmagel

excretory crystals

TS leaf infected by *Phytophthora*

leaf

- haustoria
- sporangium

stoma

Phytophthora

Paramecium

- cilia
- pellicle
- anterior contractile vacuole
- food vacuole
- rows of cilia
- macronucleus
- micronucleus
- oral groove
- cytoproct
- cytostome
- posterior contractile vacuole

50 μm

Chlorella

10 μm

- cellulose cell wall
- chloroplast
- pyrenoid (starch store)
- cell surface membrane
- clear cytoplasm

nucleus

Asexual reproduction in *Chlorella*

cell contents divide into four autospores, each with a thin cellulose cell wall

mother cell wall breaks open

posterior end

undulating membrane

cytoplasm   nucleus

Trypanosoma

3 μm

flagellum

anterior end

- long flagellum
- stigma
- photoreceptor
- paramylum granules
- cytostome
- reservoir
- contractile vacuole
- short flagellum
- basal bodies
- chloroplast
- pyrenoid
- pellicle bands
- nucleolus
- nucleus
- cytoplasm

Euglena viridis

100 μm

● **Figure 1.9** The structure of some representative protoctists.

and movement is by means of a variety of locomotory structures such as flagella, cilia or pseudopodia. Since the cytoplasm of freshwater protozoans is usually hypertonic to (more concentrated than) the aqueous environment, they take in water by osmosis. To counteract this, they have contractile vacuoles that act as pumps to remove excess water from the cytoplasm. However, contractile vacuoles may also be found in some marine protozoans. All types of nutrition are found in protozoans: some are autotrophic, others are saprotrophic and many are heterotrophic. Digestion of food takes place in food vacuoles in the cytoplasm. Gas exchange is by diffusion across the cell membrane. Waste products from cell metabolism diffuse out of the cell. The main nitrogenous waste is ammonia.

The economic importance of protozoa

Many ciliates are saprobionts and are vital in the recycling of organic wastes, particularly in sewage treatment. Parasitic forms, such as *Entamoeba*, which causes amoebic dysentery, and *Plasmodium*, may cause loss of life. Malaria, for example, can be devastating to the economy of developing countries, incapacitating millions of workers every year.

SAQ 1.4 _____

List **three** features shared by the four phyla classed as protozoa, and **two** features which distinguish them.

Kingdom Fungi

Fungi are obligate aerobes, which are killed in the absence of oxygen, or facultative anaerobes, which grow best when oxygen is available but are able to survive anaerobic conditions. They are found almost everywhere. They are eukaryotic organisms with a cell wall that is usually made of chitin. Fungi are not photosynthetic but heterotrophic, deriving their nutrients by absorption of organic materials.

Fungi are usually filamentous or thread-like. The individual threads are called **hyphae** which are usually multinucleate; these branch profusely, often fusing together to form a tangled mass of branched hyphae called the **mycelium**. Individual hyphae are surrounded by rigid cell walls and grow only at their tips. It is this form of **apical growth** that separates fungi from almost all other organisms, even filamentous ones.

Since fungi are eukaryotic, they have distinct nuclei each surrounded by a nuclear envelope with pores; they have chromosomes and a spindle that appears during nuclear division. Mitochondria are found in the cytoplasm and there is extensive endoplasmic reticulum (ER) *(figure 1.10)*; ribosomes are found both free in the cytoplasm and attached to the ER. The cytoplasm also contains numerous vacuoles containing storage materials such as starch, lipid globules and volutin.

The cytoplasm and organelles are surrounded by a selectively permeable, phospholipid unit membrane. The cytoplasm is at its most dense at the tips of the hyphae. The older parts are often metabolically inactive with large vacuoles in the cytoplasm. In septate species there are pores in the cross walls to allow substances in solution, including nuclei, to move freely from one section to another.

The growth of hyphae is very rapid under favourable conditions. Each hypha grows at the tip and branches repeatedly along its

● **Figure 1.10** Diagram of the tip of a typical fungal hypha (based on electron micrographs).

Suitable organic compound as a **carbon and energy** source, e.g. glucose, maltose, starch, cellulose, lignin	Source of combined **nitrogen** for protein: NH_3 + NITRATES Amino acids, e.g. alanine, cystine, 20 different ones in all	**Ions**: magnesium, potassium, phosphorus and trace elements	**Vitamins**, e.g. thiamine

Oxygen: very few can stand anaerobic conditions, and thus only grow on the surface of the medium	**Temperature**: the usual optimum for fungal growth is 25 °C. Most fungi survive between 5 and 35 °C	**pH**: most fungi prefer pH 7 and below, neutral to slightly acid	**Water**: The fungus is 90% water by weight. This must be absorbed from the environment

● **Figure 1.11** Conditions required for fungal growth.

Growth of sporangiophore

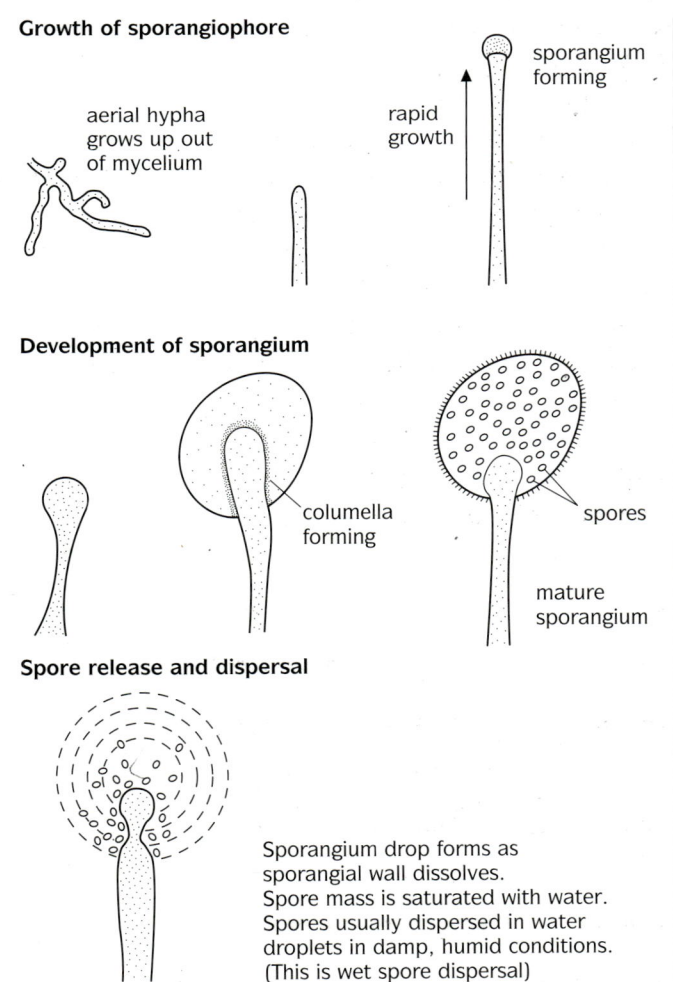

aerial hypha grows up out of mycelium

rapid growth

sporangium forming

Development of sporangium

columella forming

spores

mature sporangium

Spore release and dispersal

Sporangium drop forms as sporangial wall dissolves. Spore mass is saturated with water. Spores usually dispersed in water droplets in damp, humid conditions. (This is wet spore dispersal)

● **Figure 1.12** Asexual reproduction in *Mucor*.

length to reach new food supplies and grow away from its own waste products (*figure 1.11*).

Phylum Zygomycota (zygomycetes)

Example: *Mucor hiemalis*

In zygomycetes the hyphae are aseptate and make a large, well-developed branching mycelium. Asexual reproduction is by non-motile spores formed in a **sporangium** borne on a **sporangiophore** (*figure 1.12*). Sexual reproduction is shown in *figure 1.13*.

Phylum Ascomycota (ascomycetes)

Examples: *Penicillium notatum, Saccharomyces cerevisiae, Neurospora* spp.

All ascomycetes have aseptate hyphae. In asexual reproduction, non-motile spores, called **conidia**, are formed on special hyphal branches. Many zygotes form inside the perithecium and divide by mitosis and meiosis to form an **ascus** containing eight ascospores (four of each mating type). The ascospores germinate to form haploid mycelia when conditions are favourable.

Yeasts, such as *Saccharomyces cerevisiae*, are ascomycetes and are industrially important fungi. They have been used for centuries in the making of bread, the brewing of beer and in winemaking.

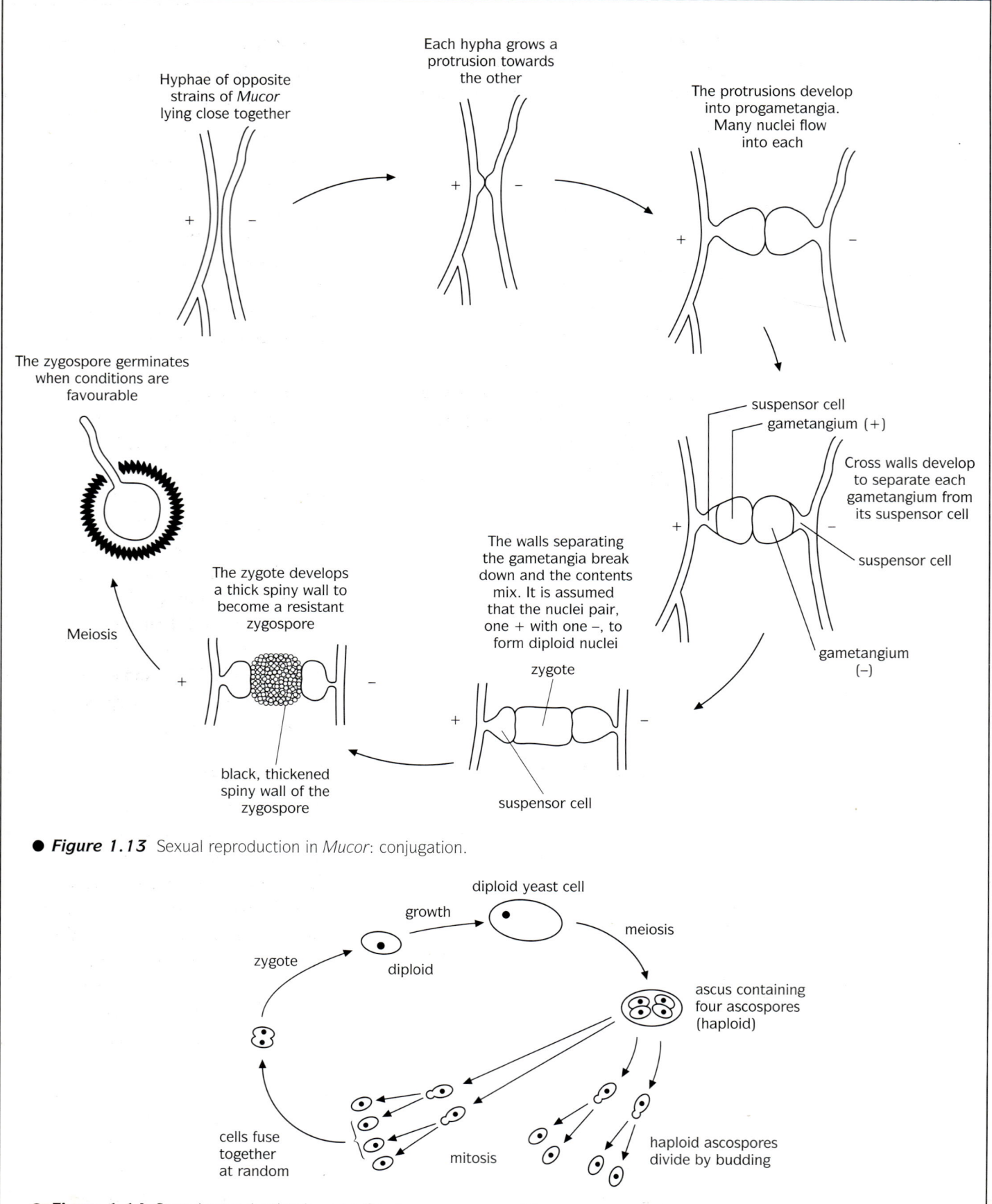

Hyphae of opposite strains of *Mucor* lying close together

Each hypha grows a protrusion towards the other

The protrusions develop into progametangia. Many nuclei flow into each

The zygospore germinates when conditions are favourable

Meiosis

The zygote develops a thick spiny wall to become a resistant zygospore

black, thickened spiny wall of the zygospore

The walls separating the gametangia break down and the contents mix. It is assumed that the nuclei pair, one + with one −, to form diploid nuclei

zygote

suspensor cell

suspensor cell

gametangium (+)

Cross walls develop to separate each gametangium from its suspensor cell

suspensor cell

gametangium (−)

● *Figure 1.13* Sexual reproduction in *Mucor*: conjugation.

diploid yeast cell

growth

meiosis

zygote

diploid

ascus containing four ascospores (haploid)

cells fuse together at random

mitosis

haploid ascospores divide by budding

● *Figure 1.14* Sexual reproduction in yeast *Saccharomyces cerevisiae*.

They are unicellular organisms, differing from other fungi in that the cell wall is composed largely of polymers of mannan and glucan *(figure 1.15)*. Sexual reproduction in yeast cells is by fusion *(figure 1.14)*.

● *Figure 1.15* Section through *Saccharomyces* cell (based on electron micrographs).

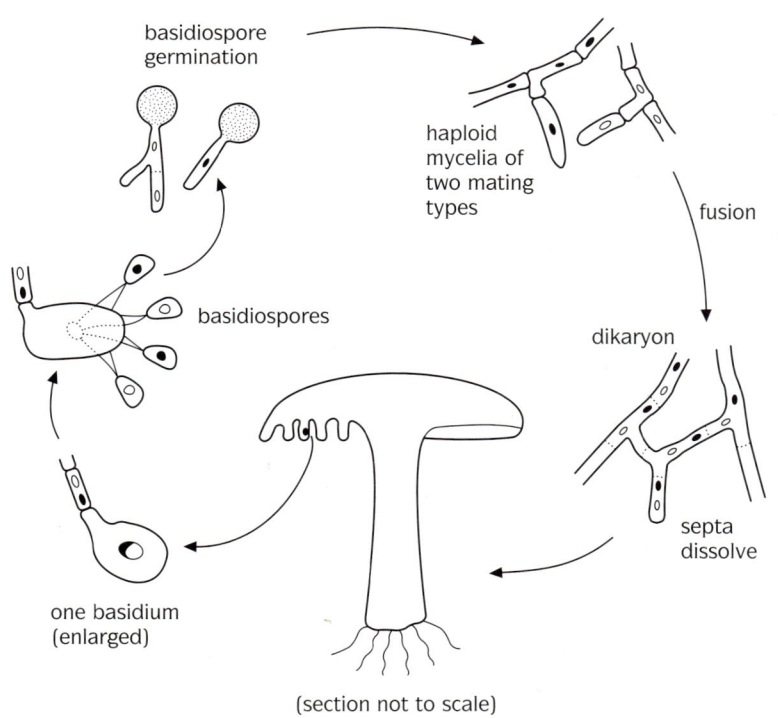

● *Figure 1.16* The life cycle of a generalised basidiomycete.

Phylum Basidiomycota (basidiomycetes)

Examples: *Agaricus campestris*, *Puccinia graminis*

All basidiomycetes have septate hyphae. Asexual reproduction is usually absent. Sexual reproduction is usually by the fusion of vegetative hyphae from two mating types. The nuclei of the two hyphae do not fuse, and the fungus exists for most of its life as a **dikaryon**, with two types of nucleus in its hyphae *(figure 1.16)*. Later a complex fruiting body is formed. This **basidiocarp** contains many **basidia** in which the nuclei fuse and meiosis takes place. Four haploid basidiospores are produced from each basidium to complete the life cycle.

The mushroom *Agaricus* is cultivated for food on a large scale. There are many other fungi which are nutritious and edible *(figure 1.17)* although some are notoriously poisonous.

Fungal spores

At some stage in all fungal life cycles, spores are produced on a specialised part of the mycelium. The spores are dormant structures though many are short-lived. They have little resistance to desiccation, ultraviolet light or predators. Vast numbers of spores are produced and dispersed. If they do not land in favourable conditions and are not destroyed they remain dormant. In favourable conditions the spore quickly swells, a germ tube grows out and the hypha elongates rapidly and soon branches. This process is called **germination**.

● **Figure 1.17** Some examples of fungi.
a Scanning EM of *Saccharomyces cerevisiae* (brewers' yeast, × 8000).
b *Agaricus* sp. (edible mushrooms).
c *Penicillium chrysogenum*, a mould used to produce the antibiotic penicillin.
d *Aspergillus niger*.

The economic importance of fungi

Table 1.5 shows examples of useful and harmful fungi.

SAQ 1.5
What are the main distinguishing features of:
a Ascomycota, b Basidiomycota, c Zygomycota?

SAQ 1.6
What features do fungi:
a have in common with higher plants,
b have different from higher plants?

SAQ 1.7
Explain the meaning of the following terms:

hypha, mycelium, septum, bud, basidium.

Some useful fungi

Fungus	Use
Penicillium notatum	antibiotic penicillin
Penicillium chrysogenum	antibiotic penicillin
Penicillium griseofulvum	antibiotic griseofulvin
Penicillium roquefortii	cheese ripening
Penicillium camemberti	cheese ripening
Aspergillus fumigatus	antibiotic fumagillin (used against amoebic dysentery)
Aspergillus niger	citric acid production
Fusarium graminearum	mycoprotein production
Candida spp.	single-cell protein from waste hydrocarbons
Saccharomyces cerevisiae	brewing, baking, winemaking
Saccharomyces carlsbergensis	brewing
Agaricus campestris	food (edible mushroom)

Some harmful fungi

Fungus	Host	Disease
Phytophthora infestans	potato	late potato blight
Rhizopus stolonifer	fruit	soft rot
Erysiphe spp.	cereals	powdery mildew
Ceratocystis ulmi	elm	Dutch elm disease
Claviceps purpurea	rye	ergot (infected rye can be fatal if eaten due to toxic alkaloids produced by the fungus)
Puccinia graminis	wheat	rusts
Trichophyton spp.	humans	athlete's foot, ringworm
Candida utilis	humans	oral/vaginal thrush

● **Table 1.5** The economic importance of fungi

Viruses

Viruses have no cellular structure. They are all obligate parasites, which means they can only reproduce when inside other living cells. They are about 50 times smaller than bacteria, ranging from 20 nm to about 300 nm and therefore cannot be seen with a light microscope. They were known to be infective agents, able to pass through filters which retained bacteria, as early as 1892. However, their structure was shown only by extensive studies using the electron microscope.

● *Figure 1.18* A generalised virus.

Structure of viruses

Viruses consist of a core containing genetic material of double-stranded or single-stranded DNA or RNA. This is surrounded by a protective coat of protein called a **capsid**, made up of subunits called **capsomeres** (*figure 1.18*). Some viruses have an envelope of lipoprotein around the capsid.

Shapes of viruses

There are three basic viral shapes as shown in *table 1.6*. These are polyhedral, helical and complex.

The life cycle of a virus

The life cycle of a bacteriophage virus, such as T2, is shown in *figure 1.19*.

Bacteriophages are important industrially because they can be used as cloning vectors, to transfer pieces of DNA to bacterial cells (see chapter 3). They are also important because they infect and destroy their host bacteria. Bacteriophage infection can destroy a fermentation process involving bacteria and

1 Bacteriophage tail fibres adsorb onto specific receptor sites on bacterial cell membrane.

2 Tail fibres bend and baseplate is anchored by pins to cell surface. Tail sheath contracts and hollow spike is pushed into cell aided by enzymes.

3 Nucleic acid is injected into bacterium with enzymes and viral proteins.

4 Phage enzymes break down bacterial DNA.

5 Phage DNA takes over control of the cell.

6 Phage DNA replicates and codes for new viral proteins.

7 New phages are assembled; lysozyme enzyme made by phage DNA.

8 Cell lysis (bursting) due to build-up of lysozyme. Phages released (up to 1000) to infect other bacteria.

Time for lytic cycle is approximately 30 minutes.

● *Figure 1.19* The lytic cycle of a bacteriophage virus.

Polyhedrons

Capsomeres arranged into multifaceted shapes. Icosahedron is the most common with 20 triangular faces, 12 corners and 30 edges, e.g. adenovirus. The herpes virus has 162 capsomeres and has an envelope as a protective coating.

Herpes virus

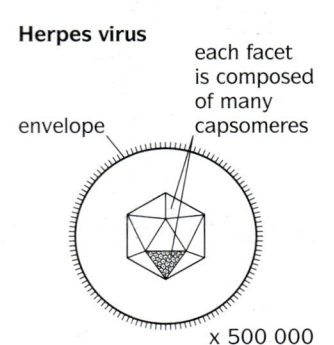

each facet is composed of many capsomeres

envelope

x 500 000

Helices

Conical capsomeres arranged helically in capsid in which RNA is embedded forming a nucleocapsid. Viruses appear as hollow rods. Some may have an outer envelope, e.g. tobacco mosaic virus, myxovirus.

Tobacco mosaic virus

helical RNA – fits into groove surrounded by protein

nucleocapsid

20 nm

Complex

More complex structure than other groups. Vaccinia (smallpox) virus has outer double membrane and inner core with DNA. Rabies virus is bullet-shaped with complex surface projections and a helical nucleocapsid. Many bacteriophages (viruses that attack bacteria) are complex.

Bacteriophage e.g. T2

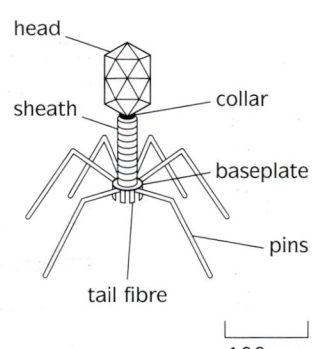

head

sheath

collar

baseplate

pins

tail fibre

100 nm

Vaccinia virus

outer membrane

nucleoid (core)

lipoprotein

DNA

inner membrane

lateral body

100 nm

● **Table 1.6** Shapes of viruses

a

viral envelope

nucleocapsid

1

2

3

4

cell surface membrane

cytoplasm of host cell

1 Enveloped virus
2 Viral envelope fuses with host cell membrane
3 Viral envelope forms part of host cell membrane
4 Nucleocapsid is released directly into the cytoplasm

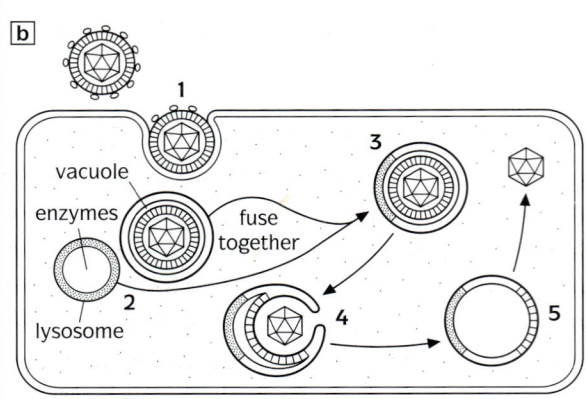

b

1

vacuole

enzymes

fuse together

3

2

lysosome

4

5

1 The viral envelope sticks to the cell membrane, endocytosis takes place and the whole virion is engulfed into a vacuole
2 The vacuole containing the virus fuses with a lysosome
3 Enzymes released into the vacuole cause the viral envelope to fuse with the vacuole membrane
4+5 The nucleocapsid is released into the cytoplasm

c

1

cell surface membrane

2

cell cytoplasm

temporary vacuole

3

endoplasmic reticulum

4

5

1 Non-enveloped virus encounters the host cell
2 Endocytosis takes place
3 The whole virus is engulfed into a vacuole
4 The vacuole fuses with the endoplasmic reticulum of the host cell
5 Virus enters endoplasmic reticulum

● **Figure 1.20** How viruses enter host cells.

a The viral envelope may fuse with the host cell membrane.

b Endocytosis.

c How a non-enveloped virus enters a cell.

● **Figure 1.21** Viruses leave the cell by a process which resembles penetration in reverse. Some viral proteins become incorporated into the host cell membrane (**a**), the virus assembles (**b** and **c**), and a 'bud' forms which is pinched off as the virus leaves the cell (**d**).

cause the loss of several days' production. The whole industrial plant may need to be closed down for thorough sterilisation.

Most viruses have a similar life cycle to a bacteriophage. However, they have different ways of penetrating animal and plant cells (*figure 1.20*) and are released differently too. A few viruses burst their host cell during release. Others leave the cell by a process similar to penetration in reverse. Enveloped viruses are released by budding, taking an envelope of the host cell membrane as they escape (*figure 1.21*).

Some viruses do not replicate once inside the host cell but instead their nucleic acid becomes incorporated into the DNA of the host cell. The virus is then known as a **provirus** since it is inactive, and the host cell is said to be **lysogenic** since it is capable of lysis once the virus becomes active (*figure 1.22*). This process is called **transduction**.

SAQ 1.8 _____
Compare the lytic and lysogenic cycles.

SAQ 1.9 _____
Do you consider viruses to be alive? Give reasons to justify your answer.

Viruses as disease-causing agents

Since viruses are always parasitic they usually cause some symptoms of disease in their host. They are of economic importance because of the loss of human and animal life caused by some types, or the inability to work due to the many less virulent types (*table 1.7*). Plant viruses cause tremendous losses in cultivated crops particularly in areas of monoculture (*table 1.8*).

Phage DNA is injected into bacterium

It becomes incorporated into the bacterial chromosome

provirus

Provirus replicates with bacterial chromosome

Cells divide by binary fission

eventually

cell division

some become activated

daughter cells

lytic cycle destroys cells

lysogenic cycle

● **Figure 1.22** The lysogenic cycle of a bacteriophage virus.

Virus	Structure	Genetic material	Disease
herpes simplex type 1 type 2	icosahedral, enveloped icosahedral, enveloped	double-stranded DNA double-stranded DNA	cold sores genital herpes
varicella zoster	icosahedral, enveloped	double-stranded DNA	chickenpox
adenovirus	icosahedral, non-enveloped	double-stranded DNA	pharyngitis conjunctivitis
variola major	complex	double-stranded DNA	smallpox
hepatitis B	icosahedral, enveloped	double-stranded DNA	serum hepatitis
parvovirus	icosahedral, non-enveloped	single-stranded DNA	viral gastroenteritis
poliovirus	icosahedral, non-enveloped	single-stranded RNA	poliomyelitis
rhinovirus	icosahedral, non-enveloped	single-stranded RNA	common cold
rubella virus	icosahedral, enveloped	single-stranded RNA	German measles (rubella)
mumps virus	helical, enveloped	single-stranded RNA	mumps
influenza virus	helical, enveloped	single-stranded RNA	influenza
rabies virus	bullet-shaped helical, enveloped	single-stranded RNA	rabies
human immunodeficiency virus (HIV)	spherical, enveloped	single-stranded RNA	acquired immunodeficiency syndrome (AIDS)

● **Table 1.7** Some viruses that cause human disease

Virus	Shape	Genetic material	Vector	Symptoms
tobacco mosaic, tomato mosaic, cucumber green-mottle	elongated	RNA	mechanical contact, grafts, fungus	yellow-brown mottled patches on leaves
cauliflower mosaic	spherical	DNA	aphids	yellow mottled leaves, poor growth
tobacco ringspot, tomato ringspot	spherical	RNA	seedborne, nematodes	ring-like patches, brown-white on leaves
barley yellows dwarf, soybean dwarf	spherical	RNA	aphids	stunted growth, yellow leaves
tomato spotted wilt	spherical enveloped	RNA	thrips	wilting leaves, discoloured spots on leaves
turnip yellow mosaic	spherical	RNA	beetle	yellow mottled patches on leaves
potato X virus, narcissus mosaic	elongated	RNA	mechanical contact or damage	mottled leaves, poor growth
tobacco rattle	elongated	RNA	nematodes	dry, brown papery leaves
beet yellows, wheat yellow leaf, beet yellow stunt	elongated	RNA	aphids	stunted growth, yellow leaves

● **Table 1.8** Some viruses causing plant disease

Retroviruses

Retroviruses are a group of viruses with two unusual features. Firstly, they have single-stranded RNA as their genetic material, instead of DNA. To infect cells they must carry the enzyme **reverse transcriptase** which converts the viral RNA into DNA once the virus starts to replicate inside the host cell.

Secondly, when the DNA copy of the viral genes is inserted into the host cell's chromosomes it forms a **provirus**. The viral infection can stay latent for some time, even several years, before the provirus is expressed to make new RNA and further virus particles. However, during this latent period, every time the host cell divides the provirus is replicated too, so that the number of infected cells increases.

Various retroviruses have been discovered in animals and humans, but the most well known is human immunodeficiency virus (HIV) which causes AIDS (acquired immunodeficiency syndrome). HIV infects T-helper lymphocytes and macrophages and destroys them. A very unusual feature of AIDS is that there is considerable variation between viruses isolated from different people, with no two viruses appearing to be exactly the same. HIV is spread in three main ways:

- by sexual contact with an infected person;
- by an infected woman passing it on to her baby through the placenta;

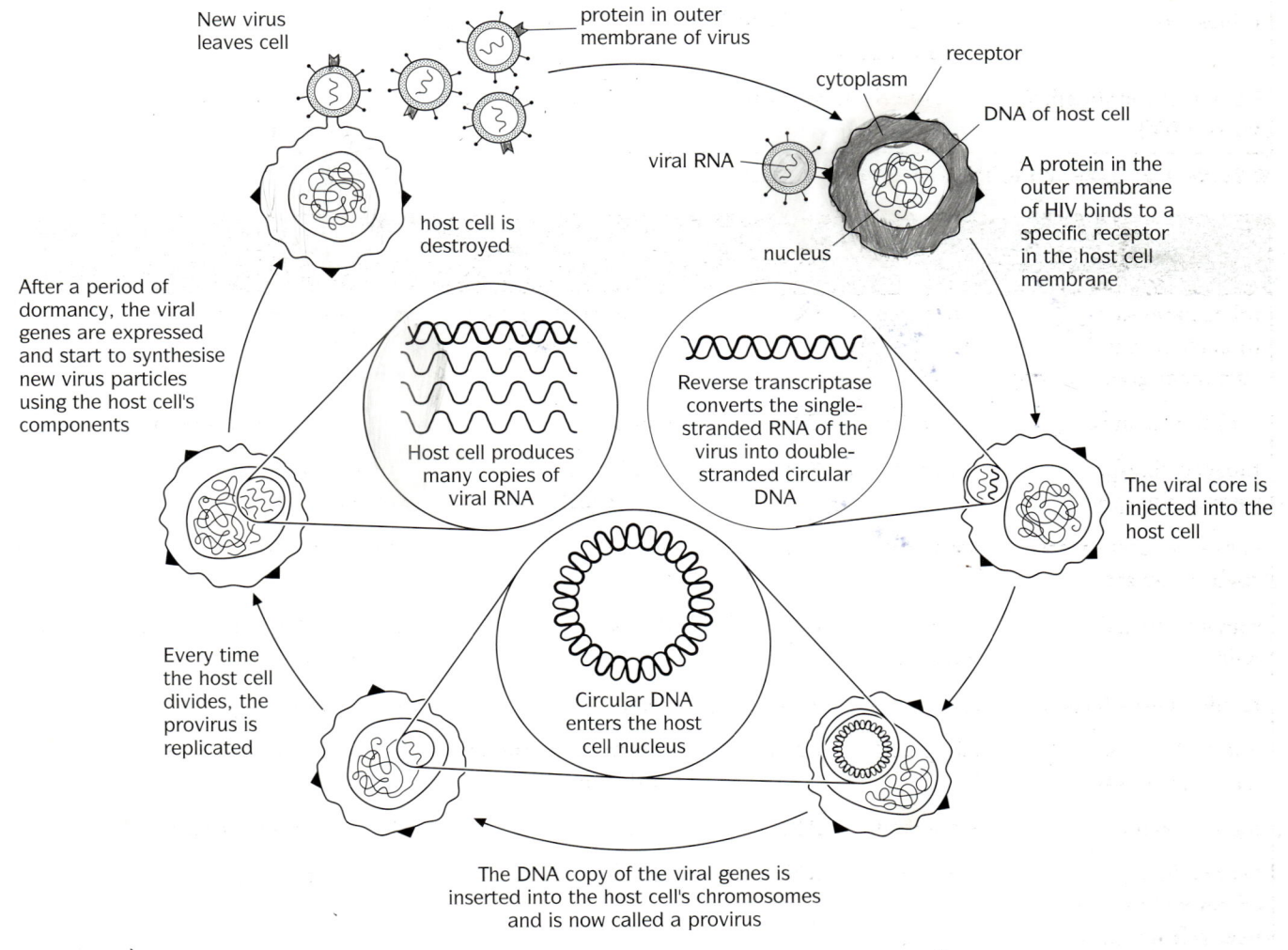

● **Figure 1.23** The life cycle of the human immunodeficiency virus.

by blood from an infected person entering another person's bloodstream, either through sharing needles, receiving infected blood during transfusion or through a wound.

HIV follows a similar pattern of infection to other retroviruses *(figure 1.23)*. While in the provirus state, it is largely hidden from the immune system. This stage can last from two to ten years, during which time the person appears healthy and feels well. After this dormant phase, the number of T cells in the body falls dramatically as infected T cells are destroyed. This marks the beginning of AIDS. The infected person's immunodeficiency means they frequently become infected by other bacteria and viruses, leading to diseases, such as pneumonia, which may result in death.

Researchers are trying to develop drugs against AIDS. Zydovudine, or AZT, prevents reverse transcriptase making DNA from RNA, while other drugs block the receptor on the host cell, preventing the virus entering the cell. Another approach is the use of recombinant DNA technology and genetic engineering to make copies of the host cell's receptor protein. These bind to the outer coat of the virus and prevent it attaching to cells. However, these drugs do not cure the condition and only prolong life and improve quality of life for AIDS patients.

Reverse transcriptase and retroviruses are widely used in genetic engineering. The enzyme is important in understanding retroviruses and in recombinant DNA technology. In the future it may be used to insert useful genes into harmless retroviruses which will transfer them to human cells. One example would be to treat babies born with genetic defects caused by a single gene, such as thalassaemia or phenylketonuria, by inserting the missing gene. Gene therapy using a retrovirus has already been used to treat ADA deficiency, which is a rare condition in which children are born with no natural immunity. Before this treatment became available, these children had to live inside a plastic bubble since any contact with pathogens could have killed them. Experimental gene therapy treatment for cystic fibrosis is already under way, though this does not use a retrovirus.

SUMMARY

- The main groups of microorganisms are the Prokaryotae (Bacteria and Cyanobacteria), Protoctista, Fungi and Viruses.

- The Prokaryotae lack a nucleus and membrane-bound organelles. Bacteria are a very diverse group, living in a range of habitats and showing various methods of nutrition. Cyanobacteria are all photosynthetic and many are nitrogen-fixing.

- The Protoctista are all eukaryotic. The group includes four phyla of protozoa, which are all aquatic, unicellular organisms with a variety of locomotory organelles; the Euglenophyta, photosynthetic, flagellated unicellular organisms; the Oomycota with aseptate hyphae, and biflagellate asexual spores; and the Chlorophyta, which are unicellular green algae.

- The Fungi are also eukaryotic, mainly with chitinous cell walls. This kingdom includes the phyla Zygomycota, Ascomycota and Basidiomycota.

- Viruses are obligate parasites which can only reproduce within living cells, so they are not classified as living organisms.

- Retroviruses are a group of viruses which have single-stranded RNA as their genetic material and use the enzyme reverse transcriptase to change their RNA to DNA. An example is HIV. Reverse transcriptase and retroviruses are important in genetic engineering.

Question

1 Make a drawing of a cell of *E. coli* based on the electron micrograph shown in *figure 1.24*. Label all the structures you can identify and annotate your diagram to explain the functions of the parts you have labelled.

● *Figure 1.24*

Chapter two

Microbiological techniques

By the end of this chapter you should be able to:

1 prepare a named medium and pour plates for inoculation;

2 inoculate solid and liquid media;

3 measure population growth by means of dilution plating, and turbidimetry and be able to use a haemocytometer;

4 dispose of cultures safely.

Laboratory safety and aseptic technique

All microbiological cultures should be treated as potentially dangerous; this will lead to good laboratory discipline. In all laboratory work certain precautions are advisable before starting any microbiological work, and aseptic technique should be used throughout the work to reduce the chance of spreading any microorganisms. These can be carried out as follows.

1 A student or teacher who is unwell should not take part in microbiological exercises. Any cuts or abrasions should be covered with a clean, waterproof dressing.

2 Always wear a laboratory coat for microbiology practical work to protect clothes and reduce the risk of contamination. The coat should be washed after use.

3 There must be no eating, drinking or smoking during practical work.

4 Windows and doors should be kept closed in order to reduce the possibility of airborne contamination.

5 Wash your hands with antibacterial soap before and after microbiological practicals.

6 Wipe down the bench with disinfectant, such as 10% sodium chlorate(I) or 1% Harris BAS cleaner, before and after microbiological work.

7 Report any spillages of cultures or breakages to your teacher immediately. Pour 10% sodium chlorate(I) on any minor spillages and leave for ten minutes before wiping with a disposable cloth.

8 Never pipette cultures by mouth, and avoid all hand-to-mouth operations, such as putting your fingers in your mouth or chewing the top of your pen.

9 Tape petri dishes securely after inoculation and label clearly with your name, date and nature of the inoculum.

10 Always work in the vicinity of a bunsen burner. Sterilise all implements before use. Metal instruments, such as wires and loops, should be heated to red heat before and after every contact with microorganisms, allowed to cool in the air for a few seconds before dipping in 70% alcohol and burning the alcohol off. Glass instruments, such as spreaders, should be dipped in 70% alcohol and the alcohol burned off. Cotton wool bungs or petri dish lids should not be laid on the bench, but held while the vessel is being used. The necks of all tubes, bottles or flasks should be passed through the bunsen flame before and after all operations.

11 Never incubate microbiological cultures at temperatures above 30 °C. Never examine live cultures of bacteria and do not open dishes of bacteria once colonies have grown. Do not isolate organisms from sources of potential pathogens, such as soil, meat, nasal secretions or lavatory seats.

12 Sterilise all media and containers by autoclaving before use. Dispose of all cultures in plastic petri dishes by placing them, unopened, in an autoclavable plastic bag and autoclave at 103 kPa (121 °C) for 20 minutes. Used instruments, such as pipettes, should be placed in disinfectant after use.

Nutritional requirements

Organisms need nutrients to generate energy and synthesise cell materials. These nutrients must be obtained from their environment. A culture medium must contain all the necessary nutrients in sufficient amount, but microorganisms have varied requirements. Their general needs are summarised in *table 2.1*.

Carbon

Photoautotrophs and chemoautotrophs use carbon dioxide as their carbon source; other nutritional groups (heterotrophs) need organic carbon (*table 2.2*). Microorganisms are so varied that there is no naturally produced organic compound that cannot be used as a carbon and energy source by at least some micro-organisms. Some individual microorganisms may be extremely versatile in their carbon require-

Energy source	Carbon source	
	Inorganic	Organic
Chemical	**Chemoautotrophs** These organisms use carbon dioxide and other inorganic materials as their energy source from oxidation or reduction reactions. Examples: *Nitrobacter* and *Nitrosomonas* in the nitrogen cycle	**Chemoheterotrophs** These organisms use complex organic materials for their carbon and energy sources. Examples: most bacteria Fungi, Protoctista and all higher animals
Light	**Photoautotrophs** These organisms use energy from sunlight to fix carbon dioxide which is their carbon source, that is photosynthesis. Examples: all green plants, cyanobacteria, Chlorophyta e.g. *Chlorella*, and some bacteria	**Photoheterotrophs** These organisms use sunlight as their energy source, but complex organic materials as their carbon source. Examples: the purple non-sulphur bacteria, e.g. *Rhodospirillum*

● **Table 2.2** The nutritional categories of living organisms

	Constituent	Functions
From water (a major component of any culture medium)	hydrogen oxygen	component of cellular water and organic cell materials component of cellular water, organic cell materials, electron acceptor in aerobic organisms
Major nutrients	carbon nitrogen sulphur phosphorus	component of organic cell materials component of proteins, nucleic acids and coenzymes component of some amino acids and coenzymes component of nucleic acids, phospholipids and coenzymes
Macronutrients (always included as salts in culture media)	potassium magnesium calcium iron	major inorganic cation, cofactor for certain enzymes important cellular cation, cofactor for many enzymes, including those involving ATP synthesis, binding of enzymes to substrates, component of chlorophylls important cellular cation, cofactor of some enzymes component of cytochromes and some other conjugated proteins, cofactor of certain enzymes
Micronutrients (often present in adequate amounts as contaminants)	manganese cobalt copper, zinc, molybdenum	cofactor for some enzymes, sometimes replaces magnesium component of vitamin B_{12} and coenzymes derived from it inorganic components of special enzymes
NB Some microorganisms have special needs not covered by this table. For example, diatoms (a type of alga) need silica for their cell walls. Sodium is needed by blue-greens and photosynthetic bacteria.		

● **Table 2.1** Requirements for the growth of microorganisms ments, whilst others can be highly specialised. For example some *Pseudomonas* species are able to use more than 90 organic compounds as their sole carbon and energy source; by contrast, certain cellulose-digesting bacteria can only use cellulose.

Nitrogen and sulphur

Some microorganisms can fix atmospheric nitrogen. Most photosynthetic organisms assimilate nitrogen and sulphur as nitrates and sulphates. Many non-photosynthetic bacteria and fungi can do this too. Some microorganisms need the ammonium ion as their nitrogen source rather than nitrate. Certain microorganisms cannot assimilate sulphate, and therefore need sulphide or an organic compound containing sulphur, such as the amino acid cysteine. The nitrogen and sulphur requirement is often met by organic nutrients, such as amino acids or peptides. These can also form the carbon and energy source.

Growth factors

Growth factors are substances which a micro-organism cannot synthesise from simpler substances and which are needed in small amounts for the cell to use in synthesising organic cell materials. They can be subdivided into three groups:

1 amino acids needed for protein synthesis;
2 purines and pyrimidines needed for nucleic acid synthesis;
3 vitamins needed for prosthetic groups or active centres of certain enzymes.

Oxygen

All cells contain oxygen in the form of water, and water is provided in all culture media. However, many organisms also need molecular oxygen, O_2, for aerobic respiration. Obligate anaerobes, on the other hand, may be killed or inhibited by molecular oxygen.

Culture media

A culture medium must contain a balanced mixture of the required nutrients, at concentrations suffic-ient to allow a good growth rate. If a nutrient is in excess, it can inhibit growth or even be toxic. Often one nutrient is present in limiting quantities, to allow adequate growth but preventing the microorganisms from multiplying at their maximum rate. By moderately slowing down the growth rate, the microorganisms are kept healthy. Usually a mineral base is made, containing all the possible nutrients in inorganic form. To this can be added a carbon source, energy source, nitrogen source and growth factors, to suit the organism being cultured. A medium composed entirely of chemically defined nutrients is called a **synthetic medium**. A medium which contains some ingredients of unknown chemical composition, such as malt extract, is called a **complex medium**.

Complex media are very good for growing a wide range of microorganisms, or when the exact nutritional requirements of a microorganism are not known. A medium may be satisfactory for initial growth, but microorganisms change the pH of the medium as they grow, because their metabolic waste products accumulate. To counteract this buffers are often added. As well as a satisfactory culture medium, factors such as light, oxygen and carbon dioxide are often necessary to meet the needs of individual microorganisms.

Selective media

A selective medium is suitable for the growth of a specific organism. This means that if you inoculate it with a mixed culture, only the specific organism the medium was designed for will be able to grow on it. Other types of microorganism will be suppressed. Such media are very specialised and are useful in diagnostic work, such as in hospitals or veterinary laboratories. For example a faecal sample containing an assortment of microorganisms can be used to inoculate selective media, such as McConkey agar containing bile salts. If any bacteria grow in this medium, which is selective for salmonellae, then the doctors are alerted to the presence of a pathogen among the many normal bacteria and can prescribe a suitable drug.

SAQ 2.1

The following is a recipe for nutrient broth, a medium used to culture bacteria.

10 g meat extract, 10 g peptone, 5 g NaCl, dissolved in 1 dm³ (litre) tap water. The pH is adjusted to pH 7.4 using molar sodium hydroxide or molar hydrochloric acid and the medium is dispensed to suitable containers and autoclaved.

a   Is this a synthetic or complex medium? Explain.

b   What is the carbon source?

c   What is the nitrogen source?

d   Suggest why tap water is used instead of distilled water.

e   Why is it necessary to adjust the pH?

SAQ 2.2

Below are two recipes for fungal media. Read the recipes, then answer the questions below.

Potato dextrose agar
■ Wash 200 g of sound potato tubers, slice and boil in tap water until soft.
■ Crush the boiled tissue in water; when cool, strain through muslin.
■ Make up to 500 cm³ with distilled water.
■ Add 20 g glucose.
■ Melt 20 g plain agar in another 500 cm³ water, mix with potato and glucose solution.
■ Dispense to containers and autoclave.

Czapek-Dox medium
0.01 g zinc sulphate, 0.5 g magnesium sulphate, 2.0 g sodium nitrate, 0.5 g potassium chloride, 0.01 g iron(II) sulphate, 1.0 g potassium phosphate, 30.0 g sucrose, 0.005 g copper(II) sulphate, 15.0 g plain agar, all dissolved in 1 dm³ (litre) of tap water.

a   For each of the two media:
   (i)   state whether it is a synthetic or complex medium;
   (ii) explain the nutritional function of each ingredient.

b   Given a fungus which will grow equally well in both media, which medium would you choose to investigate:
   (i)   the nutritional requirements of the fungus,
   (ii) the conditions necessary for spore formation,
   (iii) the effect of pH on the growth of the fungus,
   (iv) the range of carbon sources which the fungus is able to utilise,
   (v) the effect of temperature on the growth rate of the fungus?

In each case, explain clearly your reasons for choosing that particular medium.

The production of sterilised nutrient media

Nutrient agar is available in either powder or tablet form. Usually 5 cm³ of distilled or deionised water is added to each tablet, and normally two tablets with 10 cm³ of water are needed to produce a slope in a McCartney bottle or a universal bottle. The exact amount of nutrient agar powder varies with the manufacturer and different nutrient media need different amounts of distilled water. You will need to refer to the instructions on the container.

SAQ 2.3

Why, once the water is added to the tablets in the McCartney bottle, should they be allowed to stand for 10–15 minutes before autoclaving?

✳   The equipment and media to be used should be autoclaved to ensure the complete destruction of all forms of living organisms.

The total sterilisation time required varies, and the time taken is made up of three components:

1   penetration time, which is the time taken for the least accessible part of the load to reach the required temperature;
2   holding time, which is the minimum time that, at a given temperature, is known to kill all living organisms, including fungal and bacterial spores;
3   safety time, which is a safety margin and usually half the holding time.

For normal school use the total sterilisation time working at 121 °C and 103 kPa would be 20 minutes.

On autoclaving, the media will boil and enough space must be allowed so that the bubbles do not reach the plug of non-absorbent cotton wool. To prevent excessive moisture from inside the auto-clave reaching the cotton wool plug, a greaseproof paper cover held by an elastic band is placed over the plug. An alternative is to use a piece of aluminium foil.

Before use, a volume of water is added to the autoclave, normally enough to fill up to the bottom plate or trivet. The equipment and media (contained in glassware) to be sterilised are placed in a metal container or basket that rests on the trivet. The lids of McCartney bottles should be left loose so they do not explode. The autoclave lid is then securely fastened into place and the heater turned on. Steam should flow continuously through the outlet valve for about one minute to drive off all the air from inside the autoclave. The presence of any air inside the autoclave will lower the final temperature and result in impaired efficiency of the sterilisation process.

SAQ 2.4

Once the steam has built up to the required maximum pressure, excess steam will escape. Why is it necessary to turn down the heat so that the weight vibrates with only a small burst of steam?

Once the material has been autoclaved for the required time the heat is removed and the whole autoclave is allowed to cool down. To test that the pressure has returned to normal atmospheric level, the weight on the central valve should be lifted carefully. Any sign of steam or a hissing noise indicates that the autoclave has not yet cooled enough. If the weight is removed too early, before the pressure is normal and the temperature is 100 °C then any liquid in the autoclave will start to boil. This boiling can cause the medium

● *Figure 2.1* An autoclave.

to froth and stick to the bottle top or cotton wool plug, and in severe cases may boil over and down the outside of the bottle.

If the medium is in McCartney bottles, their lids should be tightened before being removed from the autoclave. If slopes are required, they should be left at a suitable angle for the contents to set. When the medium has solidified, the bottles can be stood upright. The slope increases the surface area for the growth of microorganisms. Slopes are commonly used for keeping stock cultures.

To prepare sterile nutrient agar plates

Nutrient agar is usually prepared and autoclaved in conical flasks with a non-absorbent cotton wool bung, held in place by aluminium foil or greaseproof paper and an elastic band. It is poured into petri dishes while still molten. Agar starts to solidify below 42 °C. It is best to pour the agar below 50 °C and obviously above 42 °C. A good test is to hold the

Arrange sterile petri dishes on bench. Do not open. Label on base.

1 Hold flask top in one hand and discard bung into disinfectant

molten nutrient agar

2 Flame mouth of flask

3 Mix and pour immediately into sterile petri dishes

Discard empty flask into disinfectant

4 Allow plates to set (15 min approx.)

● *Figure 2.2* Pouring sterile agar plates.

flask in the palm of the hand: when it is just cool enough to handle comfortably it is at an ideal temperature to pour into sterile petri dishes. At this temperature the agar solidifies very quickly, with little condensation on the petri dish lid.

Work in the vicinity of a bunsen burner, with a roaring flame, on a clean surface. Place the sterile petri dishes in a row and lift the petri dish lids just enough to pour in the molten agar. It should reach about halfway up each dish (*figure 2.2*). Replace the lids quickly and pass the neck of the flask through the bunsen flame for 2–3 seconds after pouring. Hold the bung between the third and the little finger during the whole operation and do not put it down on the bench, where it would become contaminated.

SAQ 2.5

When the nutrient agar has been sterilised by autoclaving, what further procedures are required to produce the agar slopes?

SAQ 2.6

The nutrient agar in the flask will cool down. At what temperature does the agar solidify and what simple test can be performed to estimate the temperature?

SAQ 2.7

Why is the neck of the flask flamed?

SAQ 2.8

When the nutrient agar is cool enough to make plates, what precautions need to be taken to reduce the risk of contamination?

SAQ 2.9

Why is it advisable not to use agar plates in which molten agar has splashed over the lid or between the lid and base of the petri dish?

Other sterilisation methods

Filtration is used for liquids that cannot be heat sterilised, such as serum, which is blood plasma with the fibrinogen removed so that it does not clot. The liquid is sucked through a sterile filter pad which traps any microorganisms. The pad is then re-sterilised and discarded.

Dry heat is effective and widely used in the flaming of inoculation loops. The nichrome loop is placed in the hot part of the bunsen flame until it glows red along its length. It is then allowed to cool without contact with any surface. Hot air methods using an oven may be used to sterilise glassware, but high temperatures and long times are needed, such as 140 °C to 180 °C for 1.5–2 hours.

Chemicals can be used, but they only kill vegetative cells not endospores. These are used to swab down benches before and after microbiological work. Various types of disinfectant are available.

Radiation is used to sterilise plastic equipment. Gamma rays are used commercially for syringe and petri dish sterilisation. Ultraviolet light is particularly effective in killing bacteria and airborne fungal spores. It is used to sterilise transfer chambers, which are special cabinets used for microbiological work in many laboratories.

SAQ 2.10

Why are plastic petri dishes and syringes not sterilised using an autoclave?

Inoculating solid and liquid media

After preparing sterile agar plates or liquid culture media, they can be inoculated with a sample of the microorganisms that are to be cultured. At all times aseptic technique should be followed.

Figure 2.3 shows the preparation of a streak plate on agar. A sterile loop is used to streak a sample of microorganisms across the surface of the agar in three parallel lines. The loop is then dipped in 70% ethanol, flamed and used to draw three more parallel lines out from the end of the first three. This is repeated three more times, after which the loop is sterilised again.

After inoculation, the lid of the petri dish should be taped on securely using two pieces of tape, as shown in *figure 2.3*. Never place the tape all around the circumference of the dish because this

1 Dip inoculating loop in 70% ethanol and flame until it glows red.

2 Still holding loop by handle, remove lid from broth culture, holding in little finger as shown.

3 Pass neck of bottle through flame.

4 Dip the cool loop into the broth culture.

6 Raise lid of petri dish with other hand, only enough to allow loop inside. Streak surface in three parallel lines.

5 Flame neck again, as in 3 and replace lid.

7 Resterilise loop and streak as shown. Sterilise loop at each 'corner'.

8 Seal dish with adhesive tape and incubate.

two pieces of tape securing lid to base

● *Figure 2.3* Preparing a streak plate.

1 Dip cork borer into 70% ethanol and flame. Cut disc of fungal mycelium. Flame cork borer again to re-sterilise.

2 Dip a mounted needle into ethanol and heat in flame. Allow to cool.

3 Pick up a disc with the sterilised needle.

CAUTION
Ethanol is highly inflammable; keep small quantity only in glass beaker, well away from the bunsen flame.

cotton wool plug

4 Still holding needle, remove plug and pass neck of flask through bunsen flame.

5 Drop disc into medium with needle, flame neck of flask again, replace plug. Re-sterilise needle.

Incubate flask for a week at 25 °C.

liquid medium

● *Figure 2.4* Inoculating a flask with a mycelial disc.

prevents oxygen passing into the dish and creates anaerobic conditions. Since many pathogens are anaerobic, such conditions are hazardous.

Figure 2.4 shows the inoculation of a liquid medium with a fungal mycelial disc.

Growth in bacteria

As bacteria are so small, it is usual to study the growth of populations of bacteria rather than individuals. Growth rate is usually measured as the increase in cell numbers over a measured period of time.

Most bacteria multiply by binary fission, which means that one cell divides into two daughter cells. In this way, the cell number doubles every generation. The time taken for a bacterial population to double in number is called the **generation time**. If conditions are ideal, some bacteria can divide every 20 minutes, although this is rare under normal conditions.

Population growth studies are essential in biotechnological industries using microorganisms on a large scale, such as brewing or producing antibiotics and single cell protein. By studying the growth of microorganisms, the ideal conditions and growth requirements can be found. If microorganisms are cultured in optimum conditions, maximum yield of the product can be obtained.

There are two forms of estimate of cell numbers in a microbial population:

1 a **total cell** count gives the total number of cells present, whether living or dead;
2 a **viable** count takes into account only living cells since these are the only cells capable of dividing.

● *Figure 2.5* Haemocytometer slide.

Total counts

These are made by sampling the culture (usually in liquid medium) at known time intervals and counting the number of cells in a known volume using a counting chamber such as a **haemocytometer** (*figure 2.5*). This is a thick microscope slide, with a slightly thinner central section designed originally for counting blood cells. When a cover slip is placed over the central section, a chamber of known depth (usually 0.1 mm) is formed. The central section is etched with an accurate grid of squares of known size. This allows for the volume of liquid over each square to be calculated. With most standard haemocytometers, this volume is $0.004\,mm^3$.

A well-mixed sample of the cell culture is usually first diluted; then it is introduced into the central chamber with a pipette, by carefully allowing the liquid to flow under the cover slip. The sample is viewed under a microscope and the number of microorganisms in several squares is counted. An average is found and, using the dilution factor, the number of microorganisms in the original sample is estimated. There is a rule used to count cells with the haemocytometer, to avoid cells which overlap the lines being counted twice. The rule is only to count cells which overlap the line on the top and left of the square; those to the bottom and right are not counted. This method is particularly useful in studying the population growth of yeast cultures and is used where there are relatively large numbers of cells in the original sample. However it is a total cell count. It does not tell us if the cells are alive or dead.

Example In *figure 2.6* there are 9 cells in the square, which has an area of $0.04\,mm^2$. The chamber has a depth of 0.1 mm, and therefore there are 9 cells in $0.004\,mm^3$. So in $1\,mm^3$ there are $9/0.004 = 2250$ cells.

If the sample from which this was taken had been diluted to a 10^{-5} dilution, then there would be 2250×10^5 cells in $1\,mm^3$ of the original sample and $1000 \times 2250 \times 10^5$ cells in $1\,cm^3$ of the original sample.

● *Figure 2.6* Total cell count on a haemocytometer grid.

Therefore the number of cells in the original sample $= 2.25 \times 10^{11}$ cells per cm^3.

Total counts may also be estimated using a colorimeter with a technique known as **turbidimetry**. Increasing the number of cells will make the culture medium more turbid (cloudy), and the turbidity is measured by the colorimeter. A culture sample is thoroughly mixed before being placed in a special flat-sided glass tube called a cuvette. The cuvette then passes before a light in the colorimeter. The amount of light which is not absorbed or scattered as it passes through the culture sample is measured to give the optical density. The more organisms there are, the greater is the optical density of the sample.

This method cannot distinguish living cells from dead ones, nor can it distinguish cells from particles of matter in the culture medium, although the colorimeter is usually set to zero before use by using a blank tube containing the culture medium alone.

SAQ 2.11

In *figure 2.7*, find the optical density of the sample: How could you find out the number of cells in a stated volume of this sample?

Viable counts

To obtain a count of live cells the culture is sampled at known time intervals, and a known volume of sample is diluted with sterile distilled water (usually to give 10^{-1}, 10^{-2}, 10^{-3}, 10^{-4}, 10^{-5} and 10^{-6} dilutions, see *figure 2.8*). Each dilution is plated onto sterile nutrient agar using aseptic technique. The plates are usually made in triplicate to increase accuracy. They are incubated until colonies are visible. Since each colony has arisen from a single microorganism, the number of microorganisms in the original sample can be calculated, taking dilution factors into account.

SAQ 2.12

Two students wanted to find out how many yeast cells were present in 1 cm^3 of a culture. Student **A** used a haemo-cytometer and calculated that there were 2.5×10^4 cells per cm^3. Student **B** made serial dilutions and pour plates, and calculated that there were 1.8×10^3 cells per cm^3. Suggest why the students obtained different answers.

Constructing a growth curve

Because cell numbers are so great, it is hard to plot a graph using actual cell numbers. Therefore, the $\log_{10}$ of the cell number is usually plotted (*figure 2.9*).

The lag phase

During the lag phase there is very little increase in cell numbers though the cells increase in size. Many factors influence the duration of the lag phase, for example:

■ if the bacteria are very inactive (such as in the spore stage) they may not divide until conditions are favourable;

■ the medium may be quite different from that on which the bacteria were growing previously, so they may need to produce new enzymes in order to digest the new nutrients.

The colorimeter measures the optical density of coloured solutions. When the coloured solution is placed in a special glass tube (a cuvette) in the instrument, light passes through the solution and coloured filter onto the photosensitive element. If the solution is dense, relatively little light passes through; if the solution is clear, more light passes through. The readings on the meter scale vary accordingly.

glass cuvette
test solution
colorimeter scale
absorbance (optical density)
transmission
photosensitive element
lamp
coloured filter

● *Figure 2.7* A colorimeter.

Aseptically transfer 1 cm³ with sterile pipette, mixing thoroughly each time

10^{-1} 10^{-2} 10^{-3} 10^{-4} 10^{-5}

Mix tube and discard last 1 cm³ into disinfectant

1 cm³ of sample

9 cm³ distilled water

● **Figure 2.8** Making a serial dilution.

The log phase (exponential phase)

In the log phase the bacteria multiply very rapidly because there is no factor limiting their growth. The supply of nutrients, oxygen and all other factors affecting growth are at an optimum, so that numbers double with each generation. For example, if the original inoculum is 10 000 bacteria cm⁻³:

after 1 generation $10\ 000 \times 2 = 10\ 000 \times 2^1$
$$= 20\ 000\ cm^{-3}$$
" 2 generations $10\ 000 \times 2 \times 2 = 10\ 000 \times 2^2$
$$= 40\ 000\ cm^{-3}$$
" 3 generations $10\ 000 \times 2 \times 2 \times 2$
$$= 10\ 000 \times 2^3 = 80\ 000\ cm^{-3}$$
" n generations $10\ 000 \times 2 \times 2 \times 2 \dots$
$$= 10\ 000 \times 2^n$$

Therefore $N = N_0 \times 2^n$
where N_0 = original number of cells
N = number of cells after n generations

The stationary phase

During this phase the population remains stable. The 'birth' rate is approximately balanced by the death rate. If nothing is added to the culture, the amount of nutrients available will now be limiting. The available substrate will provide less energy than the population requires, so the growth rate will slow down. Metabolic products may become toxic as they build up in the medium or the oxygen content may become too low for microorganisms to survive, so increasing the death rate. There may also be a change in pH of the medium, inhibiting enzyme action; for example *Lactobacillus* produces lactic acid from lactose during the souring of milk.

The death phase

In this phase microorganisms are dying rapidly while very few are being produced. Some undergo autolysis, temporarily yielding some nutrients for those microorganisms remaining alive, but the cell number falls rapidly.

Continuous cultures

✳ Bacteria grown in batch culture eventually die, as already described, due to such factors as nutrient depletion. However, bacterial cultures can be maintained indefinitely in the exponential phase. This is done by continuing to supply fresh nutrients to the medium and, at the same time, carefully removing toxic wastes and a continuous stream of the microorganisms. It is very difficult to achieve this in the school laboratory but there are many natural examples of continuous culture, the digestive system of the cow being perhaps the best example.

Growth in fungi

Unicellular fungi such as yeasts grow in a similar way to bacteria. Filamentous fungi, however, grow by elongation of their hyphae. Their form of growth varies according to the medium on which they are grown.

On a solid medium the fungal mycelium grows as an approximately circular colony across the

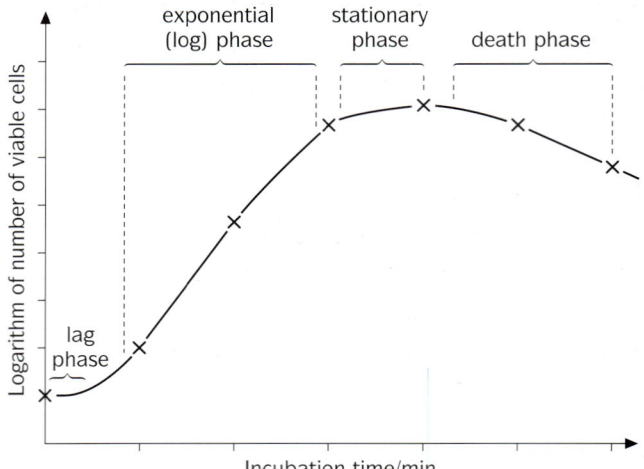

exponential (log) phase   stationary phase   death phase

lag phase

Logarithm of number of viable cells

Incubation time/min

● **Figure 2.9** Generalised growth curve of a bacterial culture.

surface of the medium. Usually the hyphae do not penetrate the medium very deeply because fungi are aerobic and rely on gaseous diffusion through the medium. Colony diameter is usually used as an index of growth.

On a stationary liquid medium the mycelium forms an approximately circular 'felt' or 'mat' on the surface. However, in a rapidly stirred liquid medium the fungus forms pellets of mycelium, which are approximately spherical and spread throughout the medium. To measure growth, the fungus can be filtered off and the dry mass obtained.

Growth curve for a filamentous fungus

Lag phase

As with bacteria, there is a lag phase when no growth occurs. There are various reasons for this:

- if a spore suspension is used as an inoculum, it will take time for the spores to germinate;
- if a mycelial disc is used, there will be many damaged hyphae which need to be repaired before they can grow;
- in either case, new enzymes may need to be synthesised before the fungus can feed off the available nutrients.

Rapid growth phase

The colony diameter, or dry mass of the fungus, increases linearly with time. However, with a fungus, growth is rarely exponential. Like bacteria, fungi grow rapidly at this time due to the presence of optimal conditions including a plentiful supply of nutrients.

Stationary phase

Growth slows down, due to the accumulation of toxic wastes, lack of nutrients, or a physical barrier such as the edge of the petri dish. Sometimes the hyphae in the centre of the mycelium undergo autolysis.

Death phase

The mycelium undergoes autolysis if the culture is maintained long enough.

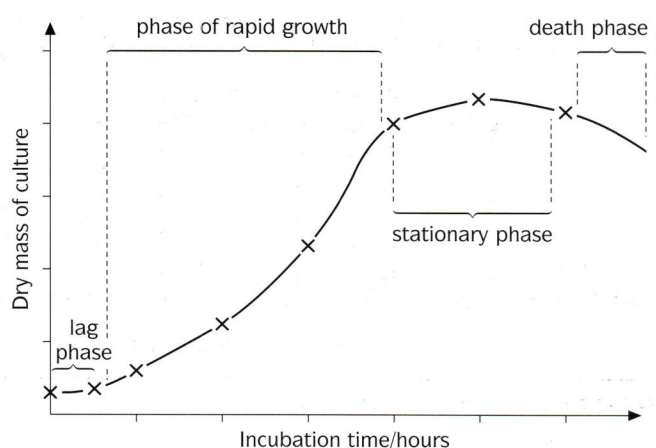

● *Figure 2.10* Growth curve of a filamentous fungus in liquid medium.

Factors affecting microbial growth

■ Temperature

All living organisms have an optimum temperature for their growth. They can be classified into three categories according to the temperature range in which they grow best.

Thermophiles have an optimum temperature above 40 °C. Thermophiles grow in hot springs, compost heaps, hot water heaters, tropical soils, hot tubs and so on. One type of bacterium has been found growing at 250 °C in the hot water streaming from a thermal vent in the ocean floor; the huge pressures at this depth prevent the cytoplasm from boiling and the bacterial proteins have extra chemical bonds to protect them from destabilisation.

Mesophiles grow best between 20 and 40 °C. Most microorganisms fall in this category, including human pathogens which are adapted to grow at 37 °C.

Psychrophiles (or **cryophiles**) grow actively at temperatures below 20 °C. These organisms grow in deep oceans, in the Arctic and Antarctic, and in fridges and freezers where they cause spoilage of refrigerated and frozen foods.

■ pH

Most bacteria grow within a pH range of 6–8 and grow best at a neutral pH of 7. Few bacteria can survive at pH values below 4. The human stomach has a pH of 1.5–2.0 which kills most bacteria. The skin and vagina in the adult are acidic to protect against infection. However, some bacteria can grow at extremes of pH, for example *Thiobacillus thiooxidans* oxidises sulphur to sulphuric acid and can grow at a pH of 0.

Fungi can tolerate acidic conditions although they grow best at pH 5–6. Fungi are very important in the decay of organic matter in acidic soils.

Microorganisms tend to produce waste products that can rapidly alter the pH of the medium. For this reason, buffers are usually added to culture media.

■ Oxygen

Aerobes require molecular oxygen for their metabolism, whereas anaerobes generally do not. Some microorganisms require a little oxygen but are harmed if too much or too little is available. Many of these need elevated carbon dioxide levels too. These microorganisms often live in parts of the human body, for example in the large intestine where low oxygen and high carbon dioxide levels are found. **Facultative anaerobes** grow aerobically when oxygen is present, but have a less efficient alternative mechanism so that they can also function in the absence of oxygen. **Obligate anaerobes** need an oxygen-free atmosphere for their growth. Some anaerobes can survive, although they will not grow, in the presence of oxygen; these are **aerotolerant**. The **strict anaerobes** are killed by even a slight amount of oxygen.

■ Carbon dioxide

Some microorganisms, including many human pathogens, grow best in elevated carbon dioxide levels.

■ Osmotic potential

Microorganisms must have water available for growth. If the water potential of the medium is higher (less negative) than that of the microbial cell, the microorganism will take up water by osmosis. In bacteria the rigid cell wall helps to resist cell lysis, but lysis can occur in microorganisms with more fragile cells. Similarly, if the osmotic potential of the environment is much lower (more negative) than that of the microorganism, water

leaves the cell by osmosis and the microorganism may die. This observation has been exploited in food preservation: high levels of either salt or sugar have been used for centuries to preserve food. Some microorganisms are adapted to grow at very low osmotic potentials; these are called **halophiles**.

■ Light

Photoautotrophs require visible light as an energy source. Some other wavelengths can be used to kill microorganisms. Short wavelength ultraviolet light may be used to kill pathogens in food shops and hospitals. X-rays can be used to sterilise medical equipment such as syringes.

■ Chemicals

Many chemicals, such as antiseptics and disinfectants, inhibit microbial growth. Antibiotics also affect microbial growth; these fall into two types, **bacteriostatic**, which prevent bacterial replication, and **bactericidal**, which kill the bacteria.

■ Nutritional factors

These were discussed earlier (page 26). Lack of any of these nutrients will limit the growth of a microorganism. Each nutrient has an optimum value which will give maximum growth. If a nutrient is supplied at a suboptimum level, there is often a linear relationship between the amount of substrate available and growth rate.

This is the basis of a **bioassay**, a valuable means of measuring the concentrations of substances like vitamins when these are very low. In a bioassay a test bacterium is selected which will only grow in the presence of the vitamin. When the vitamin has been used up, bacterial growth stops. The amount of bacterial growth will therefore be proportional to the concentration of the limiting vitamin, provided all other nutrients are available in excess. A standard curve is made, and from this the amount of vitamins in other substances can be assessed.

SAQ 2.13

Define the following terms:

obligate anaerobe, facultative anaerobe, mesophile, psychrophile.

Growth of bacteriophages

Bacteriophages replicate following the lytic cycle and the main features of this can be demonstrated by plotting a 'one-step growth curve'. A broth culture of bacteria is mixed with a suspension of compatible bacteriophage particles, such as *E. coli* with the T2 phage. Quantities are chosen so that the bacteria are in considerable excess. The mixture is incubated for a short while, to allow the phages to become attached to the bacterial cell walls. The mixture is then greatly diluted and incubated again. Samples of known volume are taken at intervals and plated onto agar. The uninfected bacteria will grow as a lawn, but infected bacteria will fail to grow and will leave a clear area in the bacterial lawn known as a 'plaque'. The plaques are counted at each stage to obtain a growth curve *(figure 2.11)*. Initially, the plaque count is constant; this is the **latent phase** following adhesion of phages to bacterial cells. As infected bacteria begin to lyse, and new phage particles are released, the plaque count rises abruptly until all the infected cells lyse. This is called the **burst period**. After this lysis has occurred, the plaque count remains approximately constant, since the diluting procedure ensures that few of the released phages will become attached to uninfected bacterial cells. The average number of new phage particles released from each infected cell is called the burst size.

● **Figure 2.11** One-step growth curve of a bacteriophage virus.

SUMMARY

■ Microorganisms need nutrients to generate energy and synthesise cell materials. These nutrients must be provided in the culture media. Selective media only support the growth of a limited range of species.

■ Various methods are used to sterilise media and microbiological equipment.

■ Growth in bacteria is usually studied by measuring population growth: either the total cell count or the viable cell count may be used. The growth curve for a filamentous fungus involves measuring mycelial growth as either colony diameter or dry mass.

■ The growth of microorganisms is affected by factors such as pH, oxygen and carbon dioxide availability, osmotic potential, light, chemicals and nutritional factors.

Questions

1 a Use the data in table 2.3 to construct a growth curve.
   b Label your graph and discuss the factors which control the growth rate at each stage.
   c The time taken for a bacterial population to double in number is called the **generation time**. Calculate the generation time for *E. coli* using the data from your graph.

2 Account for the differences in the form of growth between a fungus grown on a stationary liquid medium and a fungus grown in an agitated liquid medium.

Hours	Numbers of viable cells per cm³ medium	Total number of cells per cm³ medium
0	20 100	20 100
2	21 500	27 300
4	496 450	560 000
6	5 430 265	6 450 000
8	81 900 500	105 760 500
12	83 405 700	126 350 045
24	80 500 045	127 600 500

● **Table 2.3** Growth of a population of *E. coli* in nutrient broth

Chapter three

The scope of biotechnology

1 explain how biotechnology is used to provide both 'products' and 'services';

2 explain that biotechnology is not new, and know something of ancient examples such as brewing and bread-making;

3 explain some of the advances that have taken place in recent years;

4 discuss the development and possible future of biotechnology;

5 discuss the ethical, social and economic implications of biotechnology;

6 describe the production of novel genomes by genetic engineering.

Biotechnology is the application of biological systems, organisms or processes in manufacturing or service industries, such as genetic fingerprinting and gene therapy. It is a composite science, involving microbiology, genetics, biochemistry and engineering.

While biotechnology is a recent term, it is based on ancient technology. The brewing of beer appears to have begun in Babylon, before 6000 BC. By about 3000 BC the Ancient Egyptians were brewing several kinds of beer including 'boozah', a type of acid beer produced by fermenting a dough made from germinated barley. Their skills were passed on via the Greeks to the Romans. In medieval times, some European monasteries were well-established breweries. The first recorded tax on beer in Britain was levied by Henry II in 1188. Distilled beverages, too, have an ancient origin. In 1000 BC, distilled beverages were made in China; whiskey was being distilled in twelfth-century Ireland. Again, monasteries were particularly active in this field.

Breadmaking is another ancient technology. Remains of the Swiss lake settlers who lived ten thousand years ago show that they had developed the ability to make a kind of bread. From tomb paintings of Ancient Egypt we can tell that the Egyptians had highly developed breadmaking skills. They had made the discovery that if you leave a piece of bread dough to stand for a few days before baking, its taste and structure were improved. This was probably because of wild yeasts in the dough. The Egyptians developed the practice of keeping back a portion of the day's dough to inoculate the next day's bread or brew. By 100 BC, the Romans could buy bread in over 250 bread shops in the streets of Rome.

Cheese, wine, yogurt and vinegar have been made for centuries. More recently, in 1897, the Buchner brothers isolated enzymes from yeast, laying the foundations of enzyme technology. The discovery of antibiotics in 1929, and their large-scale production during the Second World War, created great advances in fermentation technology.

The latter half of the twentieth century has seen great advances in biology. It has become the most diversified of the natural sciences. Since the 1950s there have been many technical advances, such as the electron microscope, and these have produced a proliferation of biological discoveries. In the last 20 years, more than 20 Nobel prizes have been awarded for discoveries in this area. Perhaps the greatest contribution to modern biotechnology has been about 40 years' research into DNA. At the time, most of this research was thought to be of

● **Figure 3.1** Models of breadmaking from an Ancient Egyptian tomb.

purely academic interest, but genetic manipulation is now a central theme in biotechnology. It is this which has transformed centuries of traditional technologies into modern industrial processes.

Already, the modern science of biology has made a great contribution to the quality of human life, but biotechnology promises far more than this. Modern biotechnology offers a variety of new industries, such as mining with microorganisms, new methods of fuel production, new pharmaceuticals, new ways of using industrial wastes and new food production techniques. It attempts to solve the greatest problems facing the modern world, such as the energy crisis, food shortage, pollution and disease. Biotechnological industries generally use cheap (often waste), substrates, operate at low temperatures and consume little energy. Microorganisms are often used which can be genetically manipulated. Since microorganisms are highly versatile, with rapid growth rates, the potential for new industries is enormous.

Biotechnology is an exciting and fast-growing area, offering enormous benefits and the prospect of solving many of the perplexing problems faced by the world today. However, like so many scientific advances, there is also the threat that these technologies could be used unethically, or that people's health and welfare might be harmed unless there are strict guidelines which are adhered to.

SAQ 3.1

Which of the following processes would you consider to be biotechnology?

yogurt manufacture, bread making, producing methane from landfill sites, growing tomatoes, sewage treatment, potato crisp manufacture

Principles of biotechnology

Biotechnology exploits the chemistry of the cell to produce the chosen product *(figure 3.2)*. The cell's enzymes are used for **primary metabolism**, which means generating energy and biomass and degrading substrates, or for **secondary metabolism**. Secondary metabolism occurs at specific points in the life cycle rather than throughout the life of the organism. It is associated with changes in the organism, such as spore formation or ageing. Examples of secondary metabolites are antibiotics, terpenoids, polyketides and acetylene (propene).

The biotechnologist is able to modify the normal metabolism of the cell, so that the particular product required is made in maximum amounts.

The cell's DNA can be altered by screening microorganisms and selecting those with the best qualities. Sometimes mutation is induced (perhaps by radiation) and favourable mutations are detected by screening procedures. A more reliable, modern method is **genetic engineering**, whereby the required gene is inserted into a host cell's genome. This is discussed in the next section.

The biochemistry of cells relies on metabolic pathways to make products through a series of intermediates, where each step in the pathway is a reaction which is controlled by an enzyme. It is obvious that the enzymes must be regulated. A common regulatory

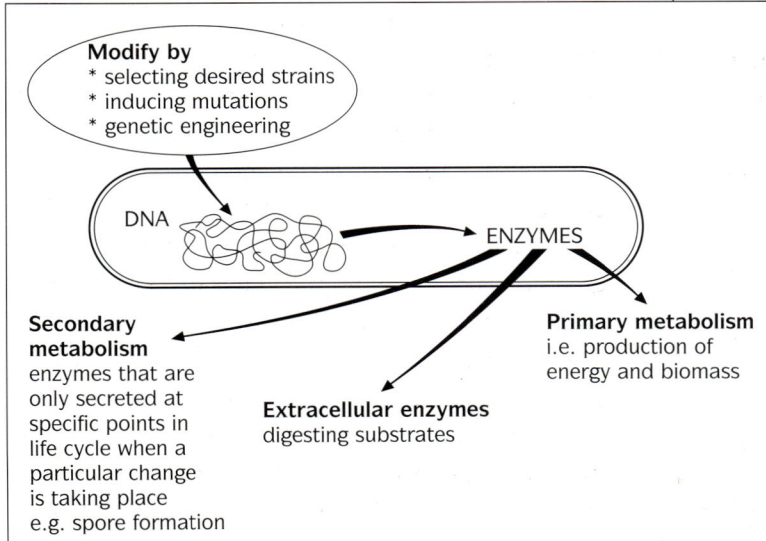

Modify by
* selecting desired strains
* inducing mutations
* genetic engineering

DNA   ENZYMES

Secondary metabolism
enzymes that are only secreted at specific points in life cycle when a particular change is taking place e.g. spore formation

Extracellular enzymes
digesting substrates

Primary metabolism
i.e. production of energy and biomass

● **Figure 3.2** Exploiting the chemistry of a cell to produce a chosen product.

● **Figure 3.3** Negative feedback.

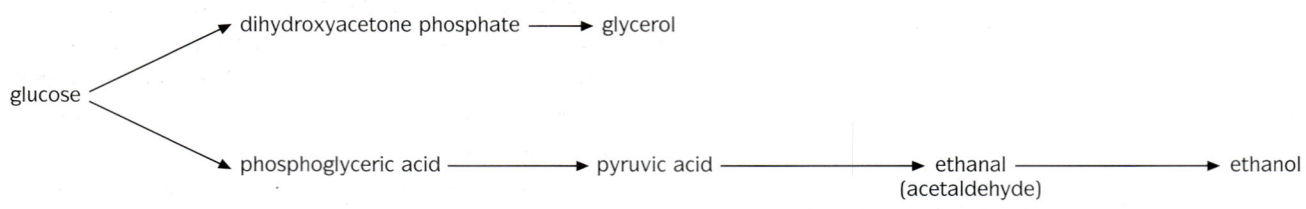

● **Figure 3.4** The production of glycerol by yeast.

mechanism in cell metabolism is **negative feedback**. For instance, in the imaginary metabolic pathway shown in *figure 3.3*, a build-up of product **D** inhibits the enzyme that catalyses the conversion of **A** to **B**, avoiding wasteful production of **B** which is not needed by the cell at that point.

Biotechnologists seek to understand these regulatory mechanisms and exploit them for maximum yields of desired metabolic products. An example occurs in yeast as shown in *figure 3.4*. This process was used in Germany to produce glycerol in the First World War. Glycerol was used to make a number of explosives such as nitroglycerine. At the start of the war, the British naval blockade prevented Germany from importing the vegetable oils they needed to make glycerol, so the Germans developed a process based on yeast. The normal fermentation pathway enables yeast to make ethanol, but if hydrogen-sulphite is added it blocks the pathway by combining with ethanal and more glycerol is made instead.

Another important fermentation process arose from the First World War. Before the war the British had imported acetone (propanone) from Germany which was required for munitions, and butanol which was used to make artificial rubber.

Since an alternative source had to be found, the British developed the acetone–butanol fermentation by *Clostridium acetobutylicum (figure 3.5)*. As well as the two solvents hydrogen gas is produced, which resulted in explosions in a number of the manufacturing plants.

The German glycerol fermentation was no longer used after the war, but the acetone–butanol process survived until the 1950s. During the Second World War the process was further developed. Semi-continuous fermentation was developed, in which *C. acetobutylicum* was cultured in a large volume of medium until growth stopped. At this stage, two-thirds of the medium was removed, and the acetone and butanol was extracted. The mixture remaining in the fermenter was topped up with fresh medium and the sugar was completely converted to solvent in 12 hours. A later development was the realisation that a non-sterile medium could be used. Although contaminating bacteria affected the yield of solvent, the saving in fuel made it cost-effective. After the Second World War, the petroleum industry became the source of these solvents and the fermentation was discontinued. However, it remains a simple process and could benefit poorer countries that cannot afford petroleum imports and have a ready supply of sugar and starch.

● **Figure 3.5** The pathway of acetone and butanol formation by *Clostridium acetobutylicum*.

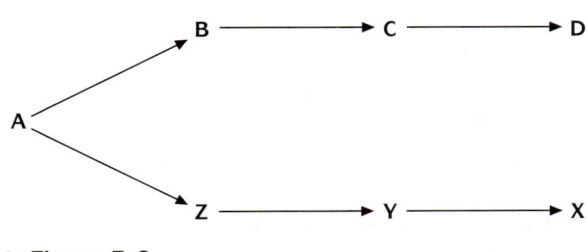

● *Figure 3.6*

SAQ 3.2

Describe how acetone and butanol could be produced in poor countries using locally available sources of sugar and starch.

SAQ 3.3

In *figure 3.6*, which shows a metabolic pathway in a particular microoganism, **X** is a useful substance which biotechnologists would like to produce in maximum quantities. Suggest ways in which they might attempt to increase the yield of **X**.

Genetic engineering

The **gene** is the basic unit of heredity: a piece of deoxyribonucleic acid (DNA) that codes for the production of a single protein. These proteins are usually enzymes, and because enzymes control the formation of many different substances, genes are able to exert a direct influence on the characteristics of an organism. A single gene which codes for a particular characteristic in this way can be passed on from generation to generation.

Genetic engineering is a means of introducing new genes into cells. The resulting cells will, therefore, have new characteristics.

In the early 1970s researchers found **restriction enzymes** in bacterial cells. These enzymes are part of the natural defence mechanism of bacteria and are released when any foreign nucleic acid enters the bacterial cell. For instance, when a virus invades a bacterium, it injects its own nucleic acid, either DNA or RNA, which 're-programs' the bacterial cells and uses the bacterial ribosomes to manufacture new virus particles. To defend itself, the bacterium produces restriction enzymes that cut the viral DNA or RNA into small fragments

which cannot 're-program' the cell. Genetic engineers have found these restriction enzymes useful for a number of reasons. Restriction enzymes are very specific and each recognises and cuts only one particular nucleotide sequence in the DNA.

Another useful property of restriction enzymes is that some of them have the ability to produce a staggered cut. This means that the fragments produced from a double strand of DNA have single-stranded 'sticky ends' protruding (*figure 3.7*). These single-stranded ends have a sequence of bases that can recognise and pair with one another. For example, the restriction enzyme EcoR1 recognises the sequence GAATTC, and cuts the DNA between G and A so that the fragments have the sequence AATT on one end and TTAA on the other. Hind III recognises the sequence AAGCTT, and cuts the DNA between the two A bases so that AGCT is on one fragment and TCGA on the other. If the fragments are brought together, provided that the conditions are right, they will join together again and can be resealed by using another enzyme called a **DNA ligase**. This allows DNA from different sources to be combined, forming **recombinant DNA**. This will happen provided that the DNA fragments are cut originally by the same restriction enzyme.

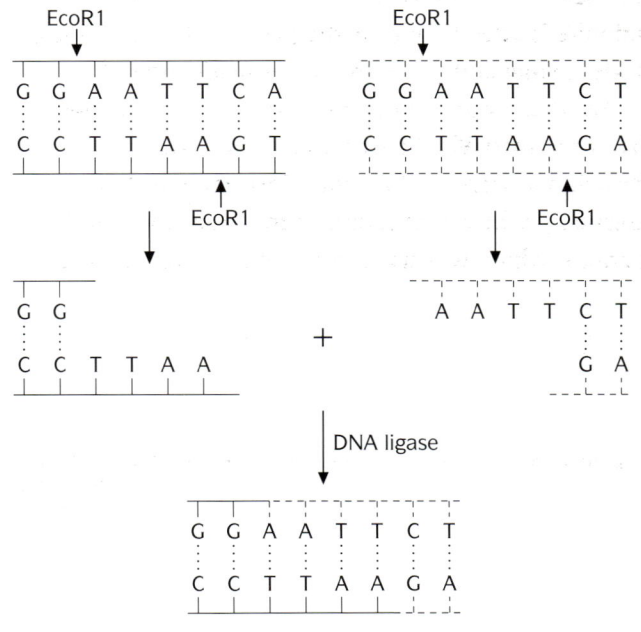

● *Figure 3.7* How 'sticky ends' are produced.

GGCATGAATCTATTAGCGAAGCTTCCCGGGATCTACTGGAATTCGCCGAAGCTTTC

CCGTACTTAGATAATCGCTTCGAAGGGCCCTAGATGACCTTAAGCGGCTTCGAAAG

● *Figure 3.8* DNA sequence for SAQ 3.4.

SAQ 3.4

Find the restriction sites on the DNA sequence in figure 3.8, where EcoR1 and Hind III would cut the DNA.

Gene cloning

The reproduction of 'foreign' genes in bacterial or other cells is called **gene cloning**, a clone being a group of cells, organisms or genes that are exact copies of each other *(figure 3.9)*. The 'foreign' gene has first to be inserted into the DNA of a culture of bacterial or other cells. The recombinant DNA is replicated as the cells divide and produces many copies of the gene.

Plasmids are circular strands of DNA which are found in many bacteria, and are separate from the bacterial chromosome. They are often used to insert foreign genes into cells. Viruses are also used.

When genetic engineering techniques are applied to microbial cells, not all the cells will be transformed. It is important that the genetic engineer can select out those cells which have been successfully transformed. This is usually done by adding a 'marker gene' as well as the gene that is required. These marker genes are often for antibiotic resistance, say tetracycline resistance. The genetic engineer can then select the transformed organisms by growing them on a medium containing tetracycline, so that all the unaltered bacteria will die.

Genetic engineering has transformed industrial processes. One advantage is that microorganisms can be genetically engineered to produce high yields, without the time-consuming process of mutation and selection. Sometimes the microorganism which synthesises a desired product is slow-growing, so genetic engineers can insert the appropriate gene into the genome of a fast-growing organism, such as *E. coli* or *Saccharomyces cerevisiae*.

Recently, it has become possible to separate the growth phase from the production phase. The cells are allowed to grow and divide rapidly at first, without producing the required product. Once the correct cell density is reached, they can be genetically 'switched on' to produce the end-product by activating a key enzyme in the synthetic pathway. This is of particular use in fermentations where the end-product is toxic.

One problem with industrial-scale fermentations is that microorganisms produce a considerable amount of heat. Cooling the fermenter is expensive, so genetic engineers try to produce a thermophilic microorganism which will synthesise the desired product.

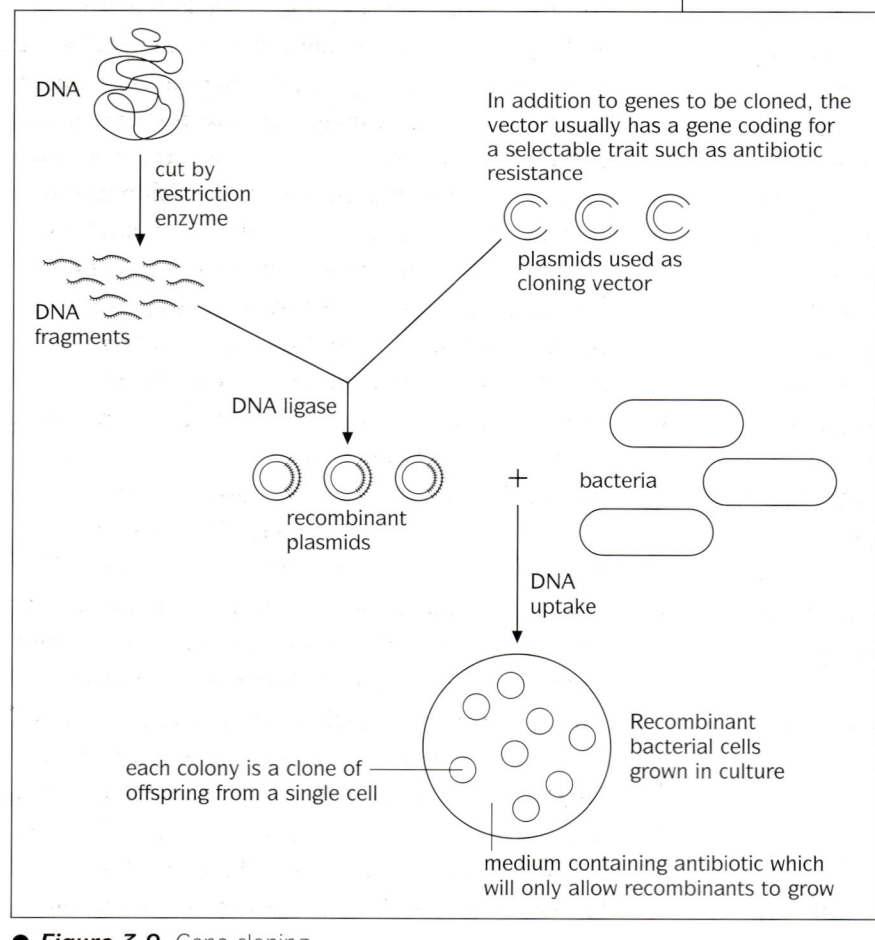

● *Figure 3.9* Gene cloning.

SAQ 3.5

Why might bacteria from hot springs or thermal vents in the ocean be of interest to a genetic engineer?

Implications of biotechnology

The law and patents

Biotechnological advances have created many legal issues. Lawyers work very differently from scientists, by examining facts in the light of existing laws, which means that new developments may take months or years to become accepted. One of the most important areas is in patent law. A **patent** is the exclusive right to manufacture or use an invention. When a scientist invents a new process or product, the scientist or the company he or she works for does not have the automatic right to the invention, unless the scientist or company applies for, and is granted, a patent. If a patent is not secured, then other scientists and companies are entitled to benefit from the invention. There are many difficulties in obtaining a patent. If the lawyers decide that the invention is not sufficiently different from other patented inventions, then a new patent is not granted. Something like a new antibiotic, or a new microorganism that could degrade a toxin previously resistant to breakdown, might well be granted a patent. When filing a patent, a fairly detailed description of the invention must be supplied which is then available for public inspection. Companies sometimes feel that publishing a patent will aid their competitors, so decide against filing a patent and keep it a trade secret instead. In 1987 the US Patent Office announced that life forms other than microorganisms could be patented, and in 1988 the first patent for a genetically engineered animal, a transgenic mouse useful in cancer research, was granted.

SAQ 3.6

Summarise briefly, in your own words, what a patent is, and explain why companies may not always obtain a patent for a new product they develop.

Herman, the world's first transgenic bull, was created by Gene Pharming Europe. He carries a modified version of the human gene for the protein lactoferrin, which is part of a mammal's natural defence against infection. Gene Pharming hope that he will pass this gene on to his female offspring, making them less susceptible to mastitis. The Dutch government have given permission for Gene Pharming to allow Herman to breed. Now the European Parliament are arguing over whether or not Gene Pharming can patent Herman's gene, and if they can charge royalties every time this gene is passed on to a descendant.

The dangers of release

Genetically engineered microorganisms are widely used in fermentation processes to make pharmaceutical and other products. Concern has been expressed about the possible dangers to workers if these organisms are accidentally released. However, these fears are decreasing since the fermentation plants can be made virtually leak-proof, and the microorganisms are killed at the end of the process. Furthermore, genetically engineered strains of *E. coli* and yeast, the two most common organisms, are not capable of inhabiting the human gut. Greater concerns are expressed about genetically engineered microorganisms which might be deliberately released into the environment. One example is the use of microorganisms to prevent frost damage to plants. Frost-sensitive plants cannot tolerate ice crystal formation within their tissues, since water expands on freezing and destroys the cell structure. Certain bacterial species which are found naturally on the surface of plants, such as *Pseudomonas syringae* and *Erwinia herbicola*, contain an ice nucleation gene which initiates ice formation at temperatures of $-1.5\,°C$ to $-5\,°C$, probably because of a membrane component. The gene for ice nucleation has been cloned and is being investigated. A strain of *P. syringae* which lacks the ice nucleation gene has been developed. If legal restrictions can be overcome, this might be sprayed on potato plants to compete with bacteria already there with the ice nucleation gene, and so reduce frost damage. The unmodified bacteria are currently being used to form 'artificial' snow on ski slopes: water containing *P. syringae* is sprayed through a fine nozzle onto a fan, and the resultant cooling produces snow.

Sometimes cultures of microorganisms are sent through the post, and concern has been expressed that dangerous or genetically modified micro-organisms might be accidentally released from a badly packed parcel. The greatest fear concerned with releasing these microorganisms is that they may proliferate in the environment. If some previously unknown hazard was discovered after the organism had been released, then there is no way that all the genetically engineered micro-organisms could be destroyed. Scientists have attempted to introduce a so-called 'suicide' gene into organisms intended for release, but this is not fool-proof, since natural selection would favour any mutants which lack the gene. However, farmers have been adding nitrogen-fixing bacterial cultures to the soil for many years now, with no detrimental effects on the environment. It is unlikely that a well-studied organism, with only two or three readily identified genes added, could become a hazard. Even so, the concerns of mutation, and hybridisation with natural microorganisms, are thought by many scientists to be largely unfounded, since exchange of genetic material occurs all the time in natural bacterial populations.

Competition with natural species

Another concern is that a genetically engineered microorganism may compete with the natural species in a habitat and ultimately lead to the loss of natural species. This has been seen in the intro-duction of animals and plants to different coun-tries, where their spread has sometimes been uncontrollable, for example the rabbit in Australia. Clearly an assessment of potential risk to the environment must be made before any genetically engineered organism is released, but there is dispute about designing a relevant test.

SAQ 3.7 _____

What type of gene do you think a so-called 'suicide gene' might be?

Some of the concerns expressed about geneti-cally engineered microorganisms do not apply to genetically engineered plants and animals, since they are bigger and therefore their spread in the environment can be monitored more easily. In particular, farm animals, which are kept in captivity, cause little concern.

There are two main concerns about plants. Firstly, such qualities as increased photosynthetic efficiency and herbicide resistance could possibly transfer into weed species through hybridisation, resulting in 'superweeds'. However, traditional plant breeding methods similarly achieve crop plants with advantageous genetic qualities which could result in this problem. The difference with genetic engineering is simply that the process is quicker. Secondly, the cloning vectors used in genetic engineering are relatives of plant pathogens. There is concern that this could result in disease transmission, should the inserted viral DNA separate from the host cell DNA. It is extremely unlikely that genetically engineered crop plants present a hazard to the environment, but neverthe-less, there are strict laws in many countries.

Genetically engineered herbicide-resistant plants also pose another problem. Many people feel that the development of these plants will lead to an increase in the use of herbicides, which are considered to be environmentally undesirable. The companies which are developing these plants claim that they hope to increase their market share, rather than increasing total herbicide use, by means of these plants. Farmers will use a specific, environ-mentally friendly herbicide when growing these plants, and the companies claim this will lead to an overall decrease in herbicide use.

New drugs

In the next decade, many more new drugs, such as viral vaccines and human proteins, will become available as a result of developments in recombin-ant DNA technology. However, since the quality of the drug rather than its mode of production is important, it appears likely that these drugs will probably not be regulated any differently from conventionally produced drugs. Indeed, many of these drugs may be safer: human growth hormone used to be produced from corpses, with the risk of transmitting Creutzfeld–Jacob disease (see page 71).

Slightly more concern surrounds domestic animals. If the animal is to be used as a source of human food, it is important that the drug does not contaminate the slaughtered animal. Bovine somatotrophin (BST) can increase milk production by 10–25% when administered to cows (page 61). Scientists in the US Food and Drug Administration have decided that the use of BST in dairy cattle presents no health risk to consumers, yet in both Europe and the USA there has been a great deal of anxiety about its use.

Gene therapy

A sample of cells can be taken from the blood or bone marrow of a patient, treated by genetic manipulation, and then replaced. One of the fears of scientists working in this field of somatic (body cell) gene therapy is that some cells harbour viruses that might act as helpers and enable the vector to spread. Also the insertion of new DNA sequences into chromosomes might activate **oncogenes**, latent genes associated with cancer. Ultimately, genetic engineering may be applied to the DNA of the cells themselves in order to treat inherited diseases. Somatic cells are non-reproductive cells, so any genetic changes produced in these cells will not be passed on to the patient's children. Only diseases caused by mutation in single genes could be treated by somatic cell gene therapy; disease due to whole chromosome defects are technically too difficult to treat.

The risks and benefits of genetic engineering on germ-line (reproductive) cells are still not clear. There are also many ethical considerations. Before considering any treatment, scientists would have to reduce the risk of a misplaced piece of DNA triggering cancer genes. The chances of interfering with an essential gene function are much higher in germ-line therapy. For example, damage to a gene coding for an essential brain function would not affect the viability of bone marrow cells or blood cells, but it would certainly affect the embryo.

There is also the risk that, in the future, germ-line techniques could be used for **eugenics**, that is to breed humans selectively. It may be possible in the near future, when more is known of the human genome sequence, to tell from a person's genes exactly what characteristics they will inherit. If gene therapy is sufficiently advanced by then, scientists may be able to alter characteristics and correct 'defects'. For some inherited diseases, such gene therapy would be beneficial. However, there may be the temptation to produce a clone of 'super-people' selected for high intelligence or super fitness.

Genetically engineered skin grafts could be a safer way of introducing genes into the human body because the cells could be removed again if something goes wrong. Genetically-engineered skin cells, carrying the gene for a human protein, have been successfully grafted on to the skin of a mouse, and the protein was secreted into its bloodstream. However, the skin cells eventually died and protein secretion stopped. If this technique could be improved, it may be possible to treat certain human diseases, such as lack of growth hormone, in this way.

Economic benefits

Biotechnology has certainly brought economic benefits, but mainly to richer countries. An example of this is high fructose corn syrup (HFCS). HFCS is produced from corn starch by enzyme conversion, firstly by hydrolysing the starch into glucose, and then by converting the glucose to fructose, which is one-and-a-half times sweeter than table sugar (sucrose). This is widely used in the USA, although tariffs levied under the European Common Agricultural Policy mean that it is very expensive in Europe. However, another biotechnologically produced artificial sweetener is aspartame, a dipeptide which has virtually no calories and is nearly 200 times sweeter than table sugar. This is greatly in demand as a sweetener, particularly in soft drinks. These sweeteners have greatly reduced the sugar imports into countries like the USA, and the reduced demand has caused the world price of sugar to fall disastrously, threatening the livelihoods of many farmers in countries like the Philippines.

Biotechnology has also improved yields of certain crops. The addition of cyanobacteria to paddy fields greatly enhances production, because of the nitrates produced by the cyanobacteria. This means that countries like India and Indonesia no longer need to import rice, destroying the livelihoods of many farmers in rice-producing countries like Thailand and Pakistan.

There have been many economic benefits to wealthier countries, where biotechnology has created skilled employment and improved quality of life in many areas such as health care. However, even agriculture may be threatened in these countries. More efficient, genetically engineered crop plants and farm animals treated with growth hormones will mean that more food can be produced in a smaller area. Healthy meat substitutes, such as mycoprotein, may reduce the demand for meat. In the future, agricultural crops may be used for a variety of purposes rather than just one. At present, grain crops are used only for food and animal feed, but they could become a source of starch for various industries and cellulose for making textiles and paper. Already, researchers at the Carlsberg company in Denmark are developing this concept. All these changes mean that smaller, less efficient farmers may go out of business.

Ethical implications

Many people feel that it is morally wrong to genetically engineer animals purely for human benefit. This argument is used particularly when genetically engineered animals are designed to suffer, such as the transgenic mouse which was developed at Harvard for cancer research. Some people feel that any food products made from genetically engineered plants or animals should be specially labelled, so that customers have the choice of whether to buy them or not.

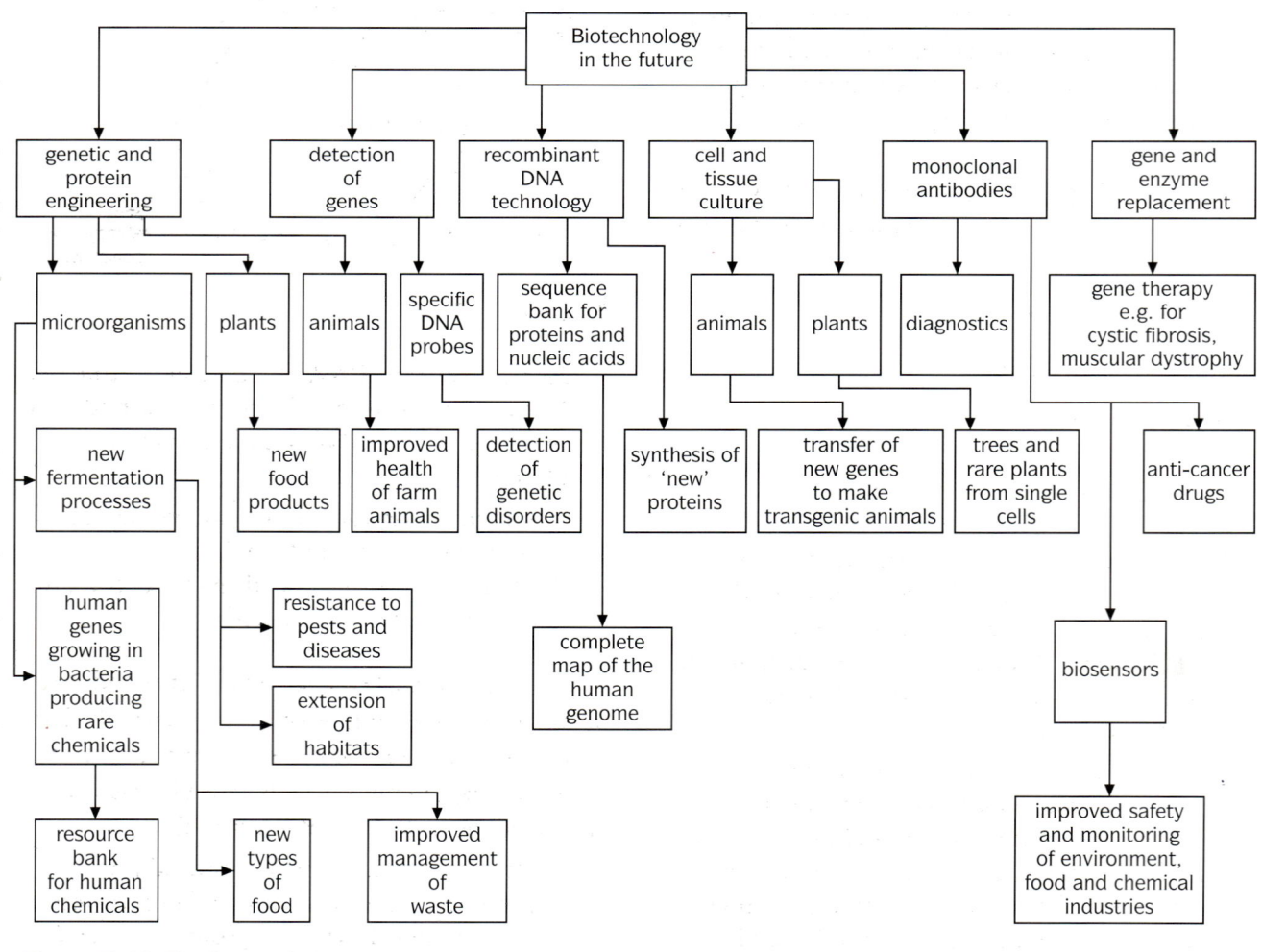

● *Figure 3.10* The future of biotechnology.

SUMMARY

■ Biotechnology is the application of biology in manufacturing and service industries.

■ Some types of biotechnology have ancient origins, such as brewing, breadmaking and cheesemaking.

■ Modern biotechnologists can exploit the biochemistry of the cell to manufacture desired products.

■ Genetic engineering may be used, whereby genes are inserted into the DNA of plant, animal or microbial cells to produce an organism with novel characteristics.

■ Biotechnological advances have created legal questions, particularly with regard to patent laws.

■ There is public concern about genetically engineered plants, animals and microorganisms, and whether they pose any risk when released into the environment. Benefits include treatments for disease and improved agriculture, although there are serious economic consequences for small farmers, particularly in poorer countries.

Questions

1 The text states that microbial enzymes can be used by the biotechnologist to generate **biomass**, **primary metabolites**, **secondary metabolites**, or that the cell's **degradative enzymes** may be exploited directly. Explain what these terms mean.

2 One strand of the base sequence in DNA recognised by the restriction enzyme EcoR1 is shown in *figure 3.11*.

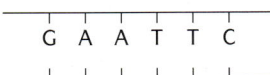

| G | A | A | T | T | C |

● *Figure 3.11*

a Write in the base sequence found on the complementary strand.

b EcoR1 cuts the sugar phosphate 'backbones' between guanine and adenine nucleotides whenever it recognises the sequence –GAATTC. Draw base sequence diagrams to show the sticky ends produced by the action of this enzyme.

Figure 3.12 is a map of a plasmid showing the positions of the recognition sequences of three restriction enzymes, Pst1, EcoR1 and Hind III. The shaded areas represent two genes, one for resistance to the antibiotic tetracycline and the other for resistance to the antibiotic ampicillin.

● *Figure 3.12*

Pieces of human DNA obtained by cutting with Hind III can be inserted into this plasmid. The pieces of human DNA are mixed with cut plasmids.

c Which restriction enzyme should be used to cut the plasmids, and why?

d What else must be added to the mixture to form recombinant plasmids?

Bacteria such as *Escherichia coli* are then added to the mixture containing recombinant plasmids. Some of these will take up the recombinant plasmids, some will take up non-recombinant plasmids, and others will not take up a plasmid at all.

e Describe an experimental procedure you could carry out, which would enable you to separate out these three groups of *E. coli*.

Questions

3 The following article appears in your local paper. A friend of yours, who does not study A level biology, asks you to explain the issues involved, and wants to know whether there is any cause for concern. What will you say to your friend?

A 'superbug' created locally to help boost world food production has prompted fears for public safety

A new microorganism developed at GENBUG Ltd's research unit has been released into local fields, it was released this week. The company claims the genetically engineered 'superbug' - capable of transforming poor soil into fertile land yielding bumper crops - is a harmless bacterium. But families living near the test fields have condemned GENBUG's 'cloak and dagger experiments' which they say 'could wreak havoc'.

John Smith, of Clover Avenue, said: 'We sussed that the fields backing onto our gardens were being used for some sort of experiment so we asked GENBUG what was going on. It turns out that freak bugs have been released into the soil. Everyone round here is blazing mad that GENBUG kept quiet about this. If we'd known before we might have been able to stop the fields being used. But now millions of mutant germs must be burrowing their way onto our land, doing God knows what long-term damage to people's health and the environment. I know scientific experiments are necessary but people living so close to these fields should have been consulted about something like this which could affect them directly.'

Mr Smith said GENBUG must have been swamped with protests. 'I've certainly made it very clear to them what I think of their cloak and dagger experiments. We still know nothing about the possible consequences.

I'm worried sick about the harm these bugs could do to my children and I know other parents round here are frightened to let youngsters play in their own gardens now. That can't be right, can it?'

A GENBUG spokesman insisted the field tests were not dangerous. He said: 'The bug we have used is an ordinary bacterium which grows naturally in the soil. But we have changed the organism's genetic blueprint (DNA) to make it very efficient at producing nitrates which plants need to grow.'

He said GENBUG chief scientists were prepared to meet residents to discuss their fears but he added: 'Our so-called superbug is quite harmless and represents no threat to the health of people living in the area. Indeed, GENBUG is proud of its amazing breakthrough in genetic engineering which could well revolutionise farming and play an important role in famine relief.'

4 Anandra Chakrabarty developed a strain of *Pseudomonas* bacterium which carried four different plasmids and could therefore degrade four different components in oil. This made it very efficient at cleaning up oil spills, so he applied for a patent on this bacterium. After much argument, the patent was eventually granted.

A doctor was treating a man from Los Angeles who had hairy cell leukaemia. The doctor removed the patient's spleen and cultured some of the cells artificially. He found that the cells produced several interesting proteins, so he patented the cells and made a considerable amount of money from commercial firms. When the patient discovered that the doctor had obtained a patent on some of his cells, he sued the doctor, but his claim was rejected. The patient is appealing against the decision.

a Is it right to patent living organisms and tissues?

b Who owns human cells and tissues? Is it the person from whose body they come, or the doctor with the skills to recognise their value?

c Drug companies can charge high prices for their drugs because they own patents, and many people are prepared to buy the drugs because they are desperate to overcome life-threatening disease. Is this morally justified? On the other hand, if companies are not granted patents, how can they recover their considerable research and development costs?

Chapter four

Large-scale production

By the end of this chapter you should be able to:

1 describe the safety requirements and working environment necessary for laboratories that work with microorganisms;

2 design and carry out experiments to show the effects of varying conditions on the growth of microorganisms;

3 describe and explain the major problems involved in large-scale fermentation processes as opposed to laboratory production;

4 describe, in outline, the principles of large-scale production illustrated by the production of penicillin.

At the beginning of chapter 2, safety guidelines were given for working with microorganisms in the school laboratory. In industry similar safety precautions are necessary, though they are even more strict.

Safety in industrial microbiology

Industrial and research laboratories have a very strict set of guidelines to follow for microbiological work. Laboratory surfaces, such as floors, working surfaces and walls must be smooth and easy to clean. There must be a regular routine of cleaning and maintenance. Some areas are

● *Figure 4.1* Clean room and protective clothing.

designated 'clean zones' where full protective clothing must be worn, and careful techniques used to avoid the escape of pathogens or the introduction of contaminating organisms into pure cultures. Often, laminar flow cabinets are used to create a sterile working area. These have air flow hoods which create a more negative air pressure within the cabinet than in the laboratory. This minimises the chances of microorganisms being carried into the laboratory in air currents. The air flow hood filters all air entering and leaving the cabinet.

SAQ 4.1

In many microbiology laboratories there are two doors present at the entrance to provide an air lock. What is the advantage of having such an air lock?

In recent years there have been concerns expressed about the potential hazards in the use of genetically engineered organisms, particularly if they are released into the environment. Evidence to date shows that recombinant organisms are no more dangerous than traditional ones. However, it is wise for research establishments and companies involved in biotechnology to be extremely careful and be aware of public concerns when designing production facilities.

The fermentation vessel should be designed to keep contaminating organisms out and therefore it should also be effective in retaining any potential pathogens. There are design features on the fermenters, such as double mechanical seals on the agitator shafts and filters on the exhaust gas outlets to help ensure that this is the case. The sampling outlets (ports) must be carefully designed to contain any spillage and must avoid the formation of aerosols. Aerosols are a risk because they provide a moist, oxygen-rich environment which encourages the growth of microorganisms. Aerosols can be inhaled and so are an easy route of infection. They can also spray microorganisms over a considerable distance where they can contaminate equipment and laboratory personnel. All effluent from the fermenter and the washings from the cleaning process must be passed through a continuous steriliser or passed into a large 'kill' tank where disinfectants are added to destroy any remaining microorganisms.

There may also be hazards involved in downstream processing, that is the processes required to obtain the product from the contents of the fermenter. Care needs to be taken with heat exchangers to avoid freezing the culture fluid which could result in thermal expansion and fracture of the exchanger. Centrifuges are notorious for producing aerosols. They must have an air-tight seal and all vents on them should be fitted with microbiological

● *Figure 4.2* Small-scale industrial fermentation.

filters. All the equipment must be connected with high quality piping and all joints securely welded. It should be possible to sterilise the whole of the fermenter and downstream processing equipment, usually with steam under pressure.

Aseptic operation

For a successful fermentation, it is vital that there should be no contamination of the culture. For this reason the entire fermenter, all ancillary equipment and the growth medium must be sterile before inoculation. The air supplied during the fermentation must be sterile and there must be no mechanical breaks in the fermenter which might allow microorganisms to enter.

All equipment is cleaned with hot water before use and then sterilised *in situ* with steam. The steam must be able to reach all parts of the fermenter assembly so the design of the fermenter is vital to avoid pockets of air which may occur if valves are incorrectly sited. All the interior surfaces should be polished since rough surfaces can act as a reservoir for contaminating microorganisms.

The culture medium, which can be several thousand dm^3 (litres), may be heat sterilised in the fermenter itself by passing steam through the cooling coils and jacket. Alternatively the medium may be prepared in a separate vessel and passed through a continuous steriliser.

All additives, for example an antifoaming agent, must also be sterilised, though strong acids or alkalis added to adjust the pH do not need sterilisation. The air supply to the culture medium is sterilised by filtration. Many types of filter materials have been developed to trap microorganisms. Bacteria and fungi are removed by filtration. However, bacteriophages in the air cannot be removed this way and their presence could result in the loss of an entire culture. In some cases, therefore, the air is heated to inactivate any bacteriophages and then cooled again before it enters the vessel. A fermentation plant designed for the large-scale production of human growth hormone or of insulin, both of which use recombinant *E. coli*, must not be situated downwind of a farmyard or sewage plant which are both rich sources of coliphages (bacteriophages which infect *E. coli*).

SAQ 4.2

Why are bacteriophages a serious problem, if they infect an industrial fermenter?

Air leaving the fermenter must also be sterilised, particularly if recombinant organisms are being grown. Not only is this a safety requirement, but it also prevents key microbial strains from becoming available to competitors. Filtration is used to sterilise the air.

The point at which the agitator/impeller drive-shaft enters the vessel is a potential source of contamination, so double mechanical seals are used and the moving parts are lubricated with condensed steam to maintain sterility.

SAQ 4.3

Explain the reasons for the following.

a A traditional brewery, using open-topped fermenters, provides a footbath containing disinfectant by the door leading to the fermenters.

b A yogurt factory prepares fruit by sterilising it and sealing it in large drums. The fruit is removed from the drum when required by pumping in sterile air.

c A supermarket has ultraviolet lights in its delicatessen area.

SAQ 4.4

You are asked to design a new microbiology laboratory for a local hospital. Describe **three** structural features that you would include to promote microbiological safety in the new laboratory.

Methods of fermentation

Solid substrate fermentation

This is probably the oldest method of fermentation, and involves growing microorganisms on a solid or semi-solid substrate. Examples are growing mushrooms on compost, breadmaking, silage production, cheese production, sauerkraut and tempe kedele (fermented soybean curd) production. Non-food examples include the production of methane from sewage sludge and other waste.

Aqueous fermentation

This refers to fermentation in a substrate which has a high water content. There are two methods of aqueous fermentation: batch and continuous fermentation.

Batch fermentation

This is carried out in a **closed** fermenter (*figure 4.3*). The microorganism is put into the fermenter with a nutrient medium and left for the fermentation to

● *Figure 4.3* Section through a batch fermenter.

take place. The product is separated from the rest of the mixture at the end. While the process is going on, nothing is added to the vessel and nothing is removed, except for the venting of waste gases. A typical growth curve for a batch fermentation is shown in *figure 2.9*, page 34. Note that all nutrients are depleted at the end of the fermentation.

During a batch fermentation environmental factors are constantly changing, although temperature is usually controlled. The phase of exponential growth lasts for only a short time.

A variation on batch fermentation is a **fed-batch process**, where nutrients are added at intervals during the fermentation.

Advantages of a batch culture compared with a continuous process are that:

■ it is easy to set up and control the environmental factors;
■ vessels are versatile: they may be used for different processes at different times, enabling a manufacturer to meet market demands more easily;
■ should a culture become contaminated, only one batch is lost, so the cost to the manufacturer is minimised.

...ation

...ation takes place in **open**
... that nutrients can be added continu-
... a steady rate, to exactly balance the
...ount of product being removed. This maintains
the microorganisms in an **exponential** phase of
growth. It is vital to monitor the environmental
factors, namely pH, oxygen level, nutrient
concentration and accumulation of products, and
to keep these constant.

Advantages of continuous fermentation are that:

■ smaller vessels are needed because the process is
more productive, with the microorganisms being
maintained in exponential growth;
■ this greater productivity can be more
cost-effective.

However, there are disadvantages.

■ In practice, it is very difficult to monitor all
the environmental factors and the system can
become unbalanced. Should a continuous
fermentation break down, there is considerable
waste which is costly.
■ There can be practical problems, like foaming,
clumping of cells and microbial growth
blocking inlets.

SAQ 4.5

Look at figure 4.3. What are the functions of the following parts?

a stirrer **b** water jacket **c** acid/alkali inlet
d sterile air inlet **e** air outlet

SAQ 4.6

What shape would you expect for a growth curve of a microorganism grown in a continuous fermenter?

Setting up an industrial process

It is not always straightforward to scale up a laboratory process to a profitable and efficient industrial
process. To do this, three stages are involved.

Basic screening

The researcher uses a small laboratory flask with a
volume of, say, $200 \, cm^3$ to grow a microorganism

● *Figure 4.4* Researcher investigating conditions for producing recombinant protein in the laboratory.

which has been found to make a useful product.
The optimum conditions for growth of the
organism are determined and, if the process works
smoothly, the next stage is to scale up the process
into a bigger vessel.

Pilot plant

The microorganism is cultured in a small-scale
fermenter of 5–$200 \, dm^3$ (litres) in volume. This is
to find the optimum operating conditions which
may not be the same as they were for very small-
scale growth.

Plant scale

The microorganism is grown in a massive industrial fermenter which is thousands of dm^3 (litres) in
volume. However, there are many problems. One
important problem is in cooling the vessel. The
$200 \, cm^3$ vessel is stirred by a small electric mixer,
using only a small amount of electricity (typically
about $300 \, W$) so there will be few problems in
cooling the vessel sufficiently. If it were scaled up
directly in proportion to the vessel, the mixer
would be the size of a tower block, use $150 \, MW$
of electricity and generate enough heat to vaporise
the contents of the fermenter. So a different
method of mixing is needed.

Other problems involved in scaling up the process are that:

- the heating up and cooling down of a large volume of liquid is very slow;
- sterile conditions are vital and the fermenter must stay sterile, since the loss of even one contaminated batch would be costly;
- it is more difficult when dealing with large volumes to maintain constant flavour and quality;
- all the processing after fermentation, such as filtering, drying, distillation, extraction and waste treatment, must be carried out on a large scale;
- any error could lead to the loss of several days' production or even wrecked equipment.

For these reasons, chemical engineers must undertake sophisticated calculations and take into account many different factors when designing a full-scale production plant.

Antibiotics

Alexander Fleming's accidental discovery of the antibiotic penicillin in 1929 is well known. He found the mould *Penicillium notatum* contaminating a petri dish of pathogenic bacteria and inhibiting their growth. From this he isolated penicillin. However, it was not until the Second World War that penicillin was successfully produced on a large scale. At first it was grown in static liquid culture in various flasks, shallow pans and milk bottles, but this process was highly inefficient and it was not possible to produce enough penicillin to meet demand. Later, a strain was developed which would grow submerged in the medium and give better yields. Modern production of penicillin uses a mutant strain developed in the laboratory.

An **antibiotic** can be defined as 'a chemical substance produced by a microorganism that, in dilute solution, can exert a growth-inhibiting effect on other microorganisms'. This definition is sometimes considered to be rather narrow since it leaves out the sulphonamides which are synthesised chemically but operate similarly to antibiotics.

Scientists are not sure why microorganisms produce antibiotics. It seems unlikely that they produce antibiotics to fight natural enemies, as so few species possess this ability and the antibiotics are not produced until late in the microorganism's life cycle. Two theories have been proposed to explain antibiotic production.

1 Antibiotics are secondary metabolites, so they may be produced to keep enzyme systems operative when the microorganism has run out of nutrients and cell division is no longer possible. Normally, when the substrate has been used up, the enzymes of that particular pathway would be broken down. If a new nutrient supply was found, there would be a delay while the necessary enzymes were produced. It has been suggested that making a secondary metabolite keeps the enzymes active, so that the microorganism can quickly take advantage of any new food supply.

2 Antibiotic production may be a means of ridding the cell of toxic metabolic waste. Although not toxic to the organism producing them, these substances could still be highly toxic to other microorganisms. If the toxin phenylacetic acid is added to a culture of *Penicillium*, penicillin production is increased, which supports this theory. It is of course possible that both theories are correct since they are not contradictory.

The industrial production of antibiotics

The first stage of antibiotic production is screening for microorganisms which produce antibiotics (*figure 4.5*). Many such organisms have been found in soil, although other sources have also been useful.

Once an antibiotic has been found, it must be tested to find its optimum production conditions (such as temperature and pH). Chromatography and other techniques can be used to see whether one or more compounds are produced. This method also indicates whether the antibiotic is new and its chemical structure may be determined. Many new antibiotics are discovered every year, but very few are ever marketed because they must satisfy strict safety codes and must be better at killing microorganisms than ones already in use.

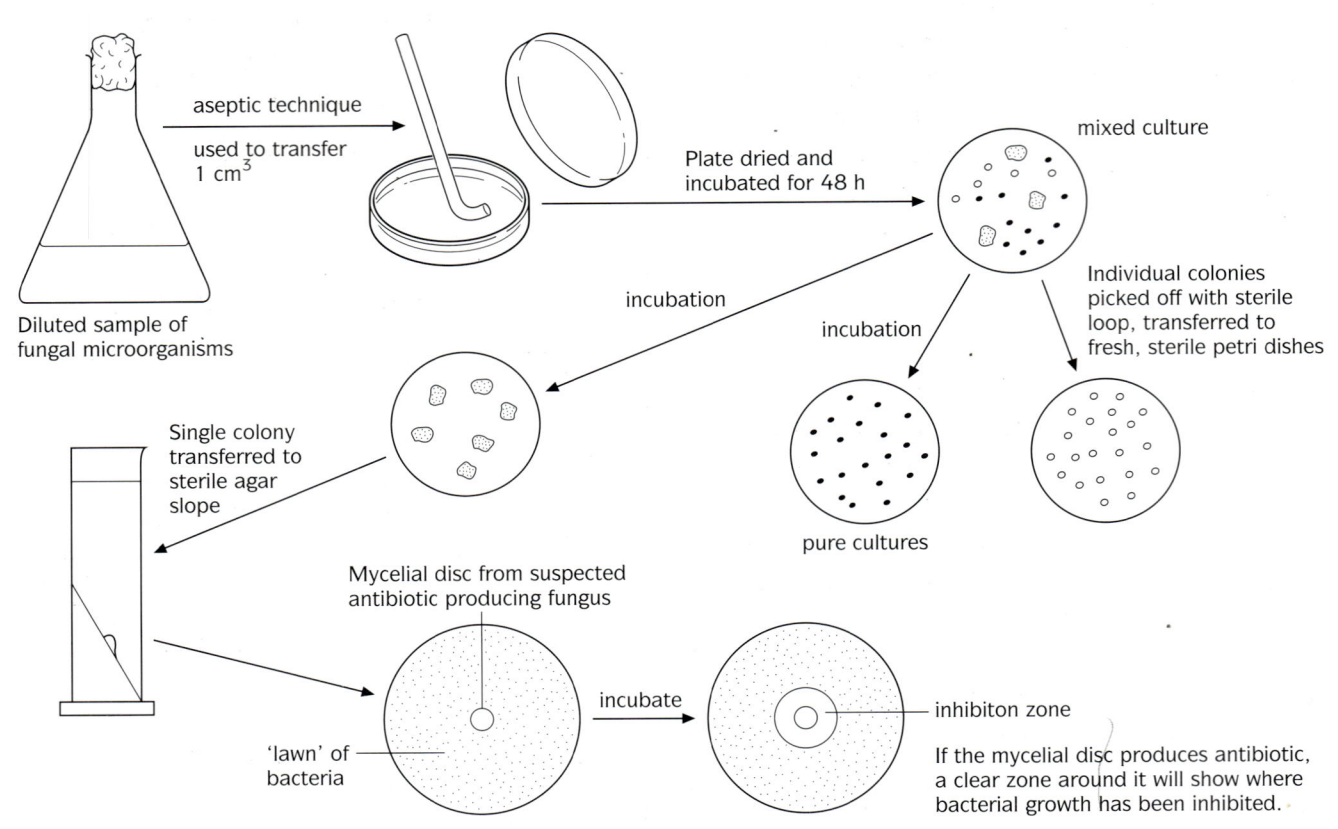

● *Figure 4.5* Screening for antibiotics in a fungus.

There are many microorganisms used in the commercial production of antibiotics. Examples include *Penicillium notatum* and *P. chryso-genum*, both used to manufacture penicillin, *P. griseofulvum*, used to manufacture griseofulvin, and the streptomycetes to manufacture streptomycin.

Commercial production of antibiotics is by **batch** or **fed-batch** culture. The antibiotic-producing microorganism is cultured in a sterile medium in a vast fermenter *(figure 4.6)*. It is grown under optimum conditions of temperature and pH (as determined by the pilot study) so that the organism grows and produces the antibiotic and secretes it into the medium. The medium contains sugar, such as glucose, together with all the

● *Figure 4.6* Commercial antibiotic production.

other nutrients the organism needs to grow, such as nitrates and sulphates. Fermentation is aerobic, so sterile air must be added to the fermenter. The fermentation is monitored so that the culture is stopped when the maximum level of antibiotic is present. The medium is then filtered off and the antibiotic extracted. The spent microorganisms are sometimes used for animal feed.

SAQ 4.7

a Suggest the purpose of the initial plate culture.

b In the laboratory scale process, the optimum conditions for growth of the microorganism are studied. What kinds of conditions might affect growth?

c In the bulk fermentation stage, these conditions need to be controlled. For each condition you have listed in **b** state how it might be controlled in the bulk fermenter.

d Suggest how the bulk fermenter, and other equipment used to manufacture antibiotics in bulk, might be sterilised.

e Why is it undesirable to keep a sample of each bulk fermentation to inoculate future fermentation runs?

f Suggest advantages and disadvantages of using antibiotic waste for animal feed.

Sometimes antibiotics are chemically modified after fermentation. All naturally occurring penicillins have a common ring structure as shown in *figure 4.7*. Different forms of penicillin have different acyl side-chains. The *Penicillium* strains first used to manufacture penicillin largely produced penicillin F. Then it was found that adding corn steep liquor to the medium caused a different kind of penicillin to be synthesised, that is penicillin G. Corn steep liquor contains a precursor of phenylacetic acid, which in turn forms the acyl side-chain of penicillin G. Penicillin G is much more useful clinically than penicillin F, so adding phenylacetic acid to the growing cultures

● **Figure 4.7** Structure of natural and synthetic penicillins.

has now become part of the production process. After this it was found that the fungi can incorporate many other chemicals into the side-chain. For example penicillin V has a phenoxyacyl group which is formed by adding phenoxyacetic acid to the medium.

It has been discovered that *Penicillium* produces small amounts of a compound which is a penicillin without an acyl group. This compound can be acylated chemically, making it possible to produce thousands of semi-synthetic penicillins, many of which have proved to be more efficient clinically than penicillin G. Furthermore, many bacteria produce an enzyme, penicillin amidase, which removes the acyl group from penicillin G. This enzyme is also used to convert penicillin G to more efficient semi-synthetic varieties.

SUMMARY

■ Strict safety precautions are necessary when working with microorganisms. This is even more important in industrial and research laboratories where pathogenic or genetically engineered strains may be used.

■ Fermenters and other equipment must be designed for aseptic operation, easy cleaning and sterilisation, and prevention of contamination and escape of organisms.

■ There are two basic methods of fermentation: solid substrate and aqueous. Aqueous fermentation may be by the batch method, which is easier to operate, or by the more productive continuous method.

■ Setting up an industrial process involves scaling up from laboratory scale, to pilot plant, before finally growing the microorganism on plant scale.

■ Penicillin is an example of a product produced industrially by either a batch or fed-batch process.

Questions

1 Antibiotics are 'secondary metabolites'. What does this mean?

2 Do you think antibiotic production would be more efficient if a continuous fermentation system was used? Explain your answer.

3 Suggest techniques which might be used to extract antibiotics from the filtered medium.

4 In a test to find out whether a newly isolated organism **X** produces an antibiotic, the following procedure was carried out. First organism **X** was inoculated onto an agar plate, along the line **AB** (*figure 4.8*). Four different known species of bacteria were inoculated along **CD**, **EF**, **GH** and **IJ**. The plate was incubated for three days. What results would you expect to see if **X**:
   a has antibiotic activity,
   b does not have antibiotic activity?

5 Describe how a bulk fermenter is prepared for the fermentation process.

6 Manufacturers of antibiotics keep a pure stock culture of the microorganism to be used for the fermentation. This stock culture is used to produce a starter culture.
   a What steps could be taken to ensure that the starter culture is pure?
   b Why would it be undesirable to keep a sample from each bulk fermentation to inoculate future fermentation runs?

7 Make a table to summarise the features of the different methods of fermentation and their relative advantages and disadvantages.

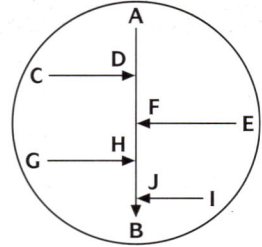

● *Figure 4.8* To find out if organism X produces an antibiotic.

Chapter five

Biotechnology in food production

By the end of this chapter you should be able to:

1 describe and explain the role of biotechnology in agriculture;

2 explain how pest resistance in crop plants may be improved by genetic engineering;

3 describe how hormones such as bovine somatotrophin (BST) may be used to increase productivity;

4 explain the use of microorganisms in the production of novel foods such as mycoprotein;

5 describe the use of by-products from biotechnology as food sources, such as yeast extract;

6 describe and explain the role of biotechnology in the manufacture of yogurt, bread and alcohol on a large scale;

7 outline how enzymes are used in fruit juice production and in meat tenderisation.

Biotechnology has an increasingly important role to play in agriculture. In the improvement of crop plants, for example, new strains of plants are being produced using genetic engineering techniques. The new plants may have an increased resistance to disease or pest attack or an enhanced capacity for nitrogen fixation. Genetic manipulation may also improve the shelf-life of some plant products. The quality of plant products can also be improved, for example wheat proteins and high-yielding oilseed. Techniques have been developed to culture roots and shoots of certain plants which produce useful secondary metabolites in their cells, such as food colourings and flavourings (table 5.1). Mint shoot cultures are used to produce essential oils such as peppermint.

In animals, biotechnology is used to make hormones which improve productivity. Bovine somatotrophin (BST) stimulates milk yields, and anabolic steroids may be used to increase muscle development. Genetic engineering techniques may be used to produce new breeds of animals with increased growth rates or milk yields.

Microorganisms can also be used to enhance agricultural production. An example is a silage inoculant called Ecosyl, developed by ICI. This contains a strain of the bacterium *Lactobacillus plantarum*. Silage is an animal feedstuff which is made from grass. Farmers harvest the grass and store it in silage pits or big polythene bales. Bacteria naturally present in the grass ferment the sugars in the grass to acids. These preserve the grass so that it can be fed to the animals throughout the winter when there is no fresh grass available.

However, silage made in this way is not always high quality as it depends on the nutrients in the grass and the microorganisms naturally present. Ecosyl is a fast-growing culture of lactic acid bacteria which compete well with the organisms naturally present. Farmers can apply the Ecosyl in powder form or spray it on to the harvested grass. The bacteria help the silage to ferment quickly to a stable pH. Tests show that the nutrient value of the silage is higher when fermented in this way. It is also more palatable and easier for cows to digest.

Product	Species	Application
quinine	*Cinchona officinale*	anti-malarial drug
ginger	*Zingiber officinale*	flavouring
morphine alkaloids	*Papaver* spp.	analgesic (painkiller)
pyrethrins	*Chrysanthemum cinerarifolium*	insecticide
vincristine	*Catharanthus roseus*	anti-cancer drug
saffron	*Crocus sativus*	pigment, flavouring
digoxin	*Digitalis* spp.	cardiatonic
diosgenin	*Dioscorea deltoidea*	contraceptive
rose oil	*Rosa* spp.	perfume

● **Table 5.1** Some useful plant products

● **Figure 5.1** Silage bales **a** with and **b** without Ecobale additive.

A similar silage inoculant, Ecobale, is made by ICI for farmers who make their silage in polythene bales. In addition to *Lactobacillus plantarum*, this inoculant also contains *Serratia rubidaea* and *Bacillus subtilis*. *L. plantarum* improves the quality of the silage, as already described, while *S. rubidaea* and *Bacillus subtilis* inhibit the growth of moulds which can sometimes damage silage made in bales.

Improving crop plants by genetic engineering

For centuries, plant breeders have improved the yields of major food crops such as wheat, by selective breeding methods. In classical plant breeding the gene to be introduced must come from a plant that is fertile with the plant to be improved. So in wheat, for example, genetic variation can only be obtained from other wheat plants, or from very closely related ancestral grasses from which wheat has evolved. However, when wheat is crossed with

these ancestral varieties, the embryos do not survive very well. New techniques have increased the rate of genetic exchange by promoting crossing-over during meiosis. This has led to the selection of embryos with genes from more distantly related plants because they are less likely to inherit harmful recessive genes from both parents.

Before genetic engineering techniques were used plant breeders induced mutations in selected plants by treating them with chemicals or radiation. This produces a greater range of variation in the offspring from which the better plants can be selected, but it is an unpredictable, lengthy and wasteful process. Now, modern molecular biology techniques involving gene insertion make possible the introduction of foreign genes from other species, whether they are distantly or closely related. Genetic engineering means that desirable genes can be selected, isolated and inserted into plants which is a more accurate and less wasteful approach. Genes can be isolated from a whole range of organisms and then inserted into the plant using a gene-transfer vector such as a plasmid or virus. Any plant containing foreign genes is said to be **transformed**.

One widely used vector is the bacterium *Agrobacterium tumefaciens*. When this bacterium invades plant cells it causes a plant disease called crown gall, a form of cancerous growth. The bacterium has a large Ti (tumour-inducing) plasmid that becomes incorporated into the genome of the infected plant cell. Genetic engineers use restriction enzymes to insert the required gene into the Ti plasmid so that it can be introduced into the plant (figure 5.2). *Agrobacterium* has several strains so it is able to infect a wide range of plants.

At present, only single genes, or very small groups of genes, can be transferred. Examples of such characteristics are resistance to disease and to herbicides, such as glyphosate. Fields can be sprayed with the herbicide, but only the weed species die since the genetically engineered crop plants are resistant to it. Scientists working in Florida have genetically engineered a strain of wheat to make it resistant to a herbicide called Basta. They did this by injecting a DNA sequence into a callus culture.

● *Figure 5.2* Gene transfer into plants.

Breeding disease-resistant plants

Virus-resistant plants are now being produced by gene transfer. *Agrobacterium* has been used to produce tomato and tobacco plants with increased resistance to the tobacco mosaic virus. It should be possible soon to produce many more crop plants that are resistant to viral disease. *Agrobacterium* may also be used to improve resistance to the many fungal and bacterial diseases of plants by inserting genes which code for a substance toxic to the pathogen or for an enzyme which blocks an essential metabolic pathway.

SAQ 5.1

Suggest other qualities which could be genetically engineered into plants to bring about an improved strain.

Protoplast fusion is another technique used to transfer disease resistance in crop plants. Plant protoplasts can be produced by gently dissolving away the cellulose cell walls using cellulase and pectinase enzymes under carefully controlled isosmotic conditions with aseptic techniques. Protoplasts can then be fused together to form **heterokaryons**. Scientists have used this technique to transfer resistance to three major virus diseases from a naturally resistant wild variety of potato into commercial, high-yielding potato plants.

Plant tissue culture techniques can be used to grow new plants from heterokaryons (*figure 5.3*). Plant protoplasts, callus tissue, or small pieces of a plant (called an 'explant') are aseptically placed on a special agar medium containing a particular balance of plant growth regulators, that is auxins and cytokinins. Depending on the relative proportion of auxins to cytokinins, roots and/or shoots will develop. The tiny plantlets produced in this way can later be transferred to compost and grown to maturity. The main advantage of plant tissue culture is that it is highly productive, growing

When plants are grown from this callus culture, the gene sequence for herbicide resistance is passed on from generation to generation.

Another example of genetic engineering in plants is the production of new varieties which emit a sky-blue glow when stressed. The amount of light emitted indicates the nature of the stress, such as drought, wind and exposure to frost. The protein aequorin occurs naturally in a kind of jellyfish. Scientists have extracted the gene for this protein and inserted it into three plant species so far, potato, tobacco and Thale cress. The protein is sensitive to the level of calcium ions in plant cells, and stressed plant cells contain abnormally high levels of calcium ions. Scientists hope that eventually these genetically engineered plants can be positioned among normal plants to act as living biosensors.

● *Figure 5.3* Plant tissue culture techniques.

many plantlets from a small amount of plant tissue, yet it uses very little space.

SAQ 5.2

Why is it important that plant tissue culture is carried out under strictly aseptic conditions?

Breeding insect-resistant plants

In Britain alone, millions of pounds a year are spent by farmers and growers in trying to control the tremendous amount of damage caused to crop plants by insect pests. However, insect pests are even more disastrous in some other countries. In parts of Africa locusts can completely destroy a whole field of crops in just a few hours. Particularly in the developed world, insecticides have been widely used to control insect pests but this has produced problems. One problem is that the first insecticides were broad spectrum, that is they were not only poisonous to the insect pests, but also to other insects and often to humans and other animals as well. The insecticides often destroyed the natural balance of organisms in the area; for example, they also killed predators of the pest so the population size of the pest could increase further and more insecticide would be needed. Some of these insecticides, such as DDT, do not break down easily and so accumulate in animals' bodies. Animals at the top of food chains could accumulate toxic levels of an insecticide. Furthermore, rain soon after spraying washes the insecticide off the plants and may pollute streams and rivers, killing plants and animals and damaging a greater area of the environment.

Recently, insecticides have been developed which are narrow spectrum, that is they only affect insects of one species or those most closely related.

These cause less environmental damage and do not harm useful insects or other animals.

However, there are other ways to destroy insect pests which avoid the use of insecticides altogether. The bacterium *Bacillus thuringiensis* produces spores which contain a natural insecticide called the **T toxin**. If the spores are eaten by many kinds of leaf-eating caterpillars, or the larvae of flies and mosquitoes, the T toxin is broken down by digestive enzymes into toxic proteins. Only organisms with the correct enzymes are susceptible, so it is much more specific and thus safer to use than most insecticides. Useful insects, birds and most other wildlife are unaffected. There were problems though. *B. thuringiensis* does not survive well in the environment, so genetic engineers have had to clone bacteria carrying the appropriate gene which were more resistant. Many people who are concerned about releasing genetically engineered organisms into the environment find this unacceptable. So scientists have tried making an insecticide that contains T toxin by growing *B. thuringiensis*, drying it, and then applying the powder to the surface of plants. Unfortunately, this approach does not work very well as the T toxin is broken down within a few days. In addition, the T toxin is quite expensive to produce which makes it less economical to use.

Genetic engineers have attempted to solve these problems by engineering plants which carry the gene for the toxin. Scientists working at the Monsanto company have inserted the T toxin gene from *B. thuringiensis* into the Ti plasmid and thereby into a tomato plant. The genetically engineered plants have been tested and have been shown to be resistant to insect attack. However, more work needs to be done. Scientists still need to be sure that the T toxin in the plants will not harm useful insects, such as honey bees which pollinate many plants. They also want to make sure that the T toxin produced by the plant does not become altered by the plant's enzymes into a different substance which is harmful to other organisms. It is also uncertain as to whether other crops, such as wheat and maize, can be genetically engineered in the same way.

SAQ 5.3

Concern has been expressed recently about the release of genetically engineered strains of bacteria into the environment during trials for producing a natural insecticide. Describe the concerns which have been expressed and discuss their validity.

Genetically engineered farm animals

There are great possibilities for genetic engineering techniques in improving farm animals. Research is still in its very early stages but one example is Herman the transgenic bull that was discussed in chapter 3.

Another example is being developed in Australia to help control sheep tick. Ticks are external parasites which suck a sheep's blood. This can lead to severe secondary infections. At present tick infection is controlled by dipping the sheep in a chemical solution which kills the ticks on contact. Dipping has to be carried out regularly and is time-consuming. The dip can also be harmful to farm workers who have to wear protective clothing and follow a rigorous set of safety procedures.

The outer covering of an insect, and the lining of its digestive system, contain chitin which can be broken down by chitinase. A chitinase gene occurs naturally in many plants. So far, scientists have successfully introduced the gene into mice. The next stage is to see whether the gene can be genetically engineered into sheep and whether the ticks will be affected by the chitinase this way.

Bovine somatotrophin (BST)

Somatotrophin is a polypeptide normally secreted by the pituitary gland of mammals. It acts as a growth-stimulating hormone which increases the rate of protein synthesis, cell division and growth of bone. In cows, bovine somatotrophin increases milk production by diverting glucose, fatty acids and body fats to the mammary glands. Giving additional BST can increase these effects, for example the milk yield of a good dairy cow can be increased by up to 10 kg per day simply by injecting a small dose of BST into the cow every one or two weeks.

The BST for use in farming is produced by biotechnology. The gene for BST synthesis has been isolated from a cow and inserted into a plasmid from a bacterium. The plasmid is then used as a vector to insert the recombined gene into the bacterium *Escherichia coli*. The bacterium containing the recombinant plasmid is then allowed to multiply under carefully controlled conditions in a batch fermentation process. These cloned bacteria produce large quantities of BST as granules within their cells.

The bacteria are homogenised to split the cells open, releasing the granules along with cell debris. A very complex purification process then takes place, involving centrifugation and protein purification techniques to separate out the polypeptide BST from all the other cell proteins. The manufactured BST differs very slightly from natural BST because it has a few extra amino acids.

The highly purified BST is formulated into a slow-release preparation suitable for injection into cows. Very strict aseptic techniques must be applied throughout the manufacture and purification process.

Research has shown that BST increases lactation in cows but they need to eat more food. This increase in feed is offset by the value of the extra milk produced (*table 5.2*).

	feed in kg/day	*milk out kg/day*	*milk to feed ratio*
without BST	34.1	27.9	0.82
with BST	37.8	37.3	0.99

● **Table 5.2** To compare milk yield in a cow with and without BST treatment

Mastitis is a bacterial infection of the udder in milking cows. Cows with high milk yields are more likely to get mastitis, and recent studies have shown that cows given artificial BST are 79% more likely to become infected.

Apart from this, cows treated with artificial BST can conceive and give birth normally and their behaviour and temperament seem unaffected.

The Food and Drug Administration (FDA) approved the use of BST in the US in November 1993. Approval for the use of BST in the EU has not yet been granted, but there have been clinical trials.

There may be some drawbacks to its continued use. One concern is the possible risk to the consumer of drinking milk or eating meat which may have a higher than normal level of BST. The natural concentration in milk is usually around 2 parts per billion (ppb) but with treatment may be 10 ppb. BST should not be a risk to most consumers because it is a polypeptide and will be broken down to its constituent amino acids by the human digestive system. However, there is some concern about the effect of the hormone on pregnant and lactating mothers.

Other concerns are for the cows themselves. Prolonged use of BST has been shown to weaken the cow by depleting the immune system and producing an increased susceptibility to disease. Within the EU, there is already an over-production of milk. In the UK, milk quotas have been imposed on farmers to help control milk supply. So the use of BST does not have much to offer farmers except a small reduction in the size of their dairy herd farming costs could be reduced by getting the same quantity of milk from fewer cows. Alternatively, the use of BST may allow a more flexible management of milk supply. In August each year, there is a shortage of milk for cheese manufacture because autumn is a peak time for calving. BST could be given to help overcome this seasonal shortfall, rather than as a way of increasing milk supply overall.

SAQ 5.4
Summarise the advantages and disadvantages of using BST.

SAQ 5.5
Why are aseptic techniques used in the manufacture of BST?

Single cell protein (SCP)

Microorganisms can be grown on a whole range of cheap or waste materials, harvested and then purified or processed to provide food for either humans or livestock. If the foodstuff produced is a protein, the product is called single cell protein (SCP). Many microorganisms are suitable for this process, including algae, blue-greens, fungi and bacteria.

Examples of substrates available

■ The cheese industry produces large amounts of whey, much of which is wasted. Whey contains both protein and lactose, and some yeasts can grow on this waste to produce high grade protein and certain vitamins. The product is used to supplement cattle feed.

■ The sugar refining industry produces molasses. At present, some of this waste is fermented and distilled to produce rum and some is fed directly to cattle. However, yeast can be grown on molasses to give very high yields.

■ Sulphite liquor is a waste product from the wood pulping industry and contains low levels of sugar. Fungi can grow on this, although newer wood pulping methods have led to less sulphite liquor waste.

■ The oil industry burns off considerable quantities of natural gas while producing oil because it is uneconomic to use the gas. In the future it could become economic to liquefy and store the gas for conversion to methanol, which would support bacteria and yield high value protein.

■ In oil distillation straight-chain alkanes are produced as a rather waxy waste product. They are of limited use in other industries, but they can be used as a substrate for yeasts which can then form animal feed.

Advantages of using microorganisms to produce SCP

■ Microorganisms have very rapid growth rates. If conditions for growth are kept at an optimum, some microorganisms can double their biomass every 20 minutes.

■ Microorganisms can exploit a great variety of substrates, particularly wastes and other substances of low commercial value.

■ The genetic characteristics of microorganisms can be manipulated fairly easily and they can readily be screened for desirable characteristics such as high growth rate or lipid content.

■ Microorganisms have a fairly high protein content with a good proportion of essential amino acids.

■ Many foodstuffs and secondary plant products can only be grown in warm climates, but with fermenters they can be produced almost anywhere. Fermenters also require very little land area.

Problems encountered with SCP

SCP is often contaminated with the substrate, as total purification is not feasible. This creates a problem where the substrate is toxic, such as sewage or methanol. This problem can be overcome by adding an extra stage in the food chain. For example the toxic substrate is used to grow organism **A**. Organism **A** is then used as a substrate for organism **B**, which is then harvested to yield SCP.

This is safer, but as the food chain is longer, the process is less efficient due to energy losses at each trophic level. Alternatively, a product may be produced from the toxic waste and then used as a substrate for SCP. An example of this is when sewage is converted to methane by methanogenic bacteria. The methane is then used as the substrate on which to grow single-cell protein.

Another problem is that prokaryotic micro-organisms used for SCP production have a high nucleic acid content. This happens particularly where production is by continuous fermentation, since growth is exponential. Nucleic acid content is about 15% of the dry mass of bacteria, but only about 4% in meat and fish. Excess nucleic acid in human diets leads to health problems, such as kidney stones, and can cause nausea, vomiting and diarrhoea. Using chemical methods or enzymes to reduce nucleic acid levels is prohibitively expensive, so prokaryotic SCP is best used either as a human food supplement or for feeding farm animals. Eukaryotic SCP, based on algae and fungi, does not give such problems as the nucleic acid content is much lower.

Scientists must also choose the species of microorganism carefully, so that there should be no risk of pathogens being present. *Pseudomonas* is a useful bacterium which grows on various hydro-carbons and methanol. However, some related pseudomonads are pathogens and scientists are concerned that if the organism undergoes a genetic change it could cause disease. One way to avoid this is to kill the microorganism during some stage of SCP processing.

Examples of SCP production

Marlow Foods produce a product called Myco-protein by using a filamentous fungus, *Fusarium graminearum*, grown in continuous fermenters. Although Mycoprotein is technically not a single cell protein, it is often included as such because it uses the same methods and processes in its produc-tion. The substrate is a glucose solution, together with oxygen, a nitrogen source and minerals. As the fungus is filamen-tous, the product contains fibres which can be aligned to make a meat substitute. It is available as Quorn in ready meals in major supermarkets throughout the country (*figure 5.4*).

Spirulina is a blue-green bacterium which has been grown for many years as SCP. Because it is photosynthetic, it grows in ponds, needing only carbon dioxide and inorganic ions. Dried *Spirulina* has a high nutrient value and can be fed to animals. It is also gaining popu-larity as a health food.

ICI used to make a single cell protein, Pruteen, which was used as an animal feed. Work started in the early 1970s when they found a very tiny rod-shaped bacterium, *Methylophilus methylotrophus*, which would grow very efficiently using methanol and ammonia as a substrate. In 1972 a pilot plant was set up, and in 1979 an enormous

pressure cycle fermenter went into production (*figure 5.5*). Unfortunately, the process did not prove to be economic as other forms of animal feed, such as fish-meal, were cheaper. As a result, the Pruteen plant was closed down in the mid 1980s.

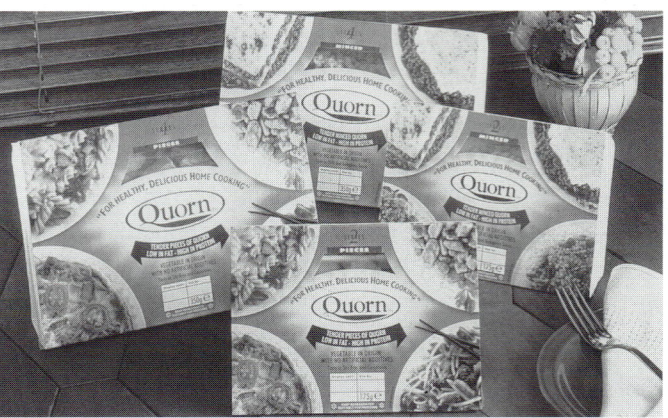

● *Figure 5.4* Mycoprotein products.

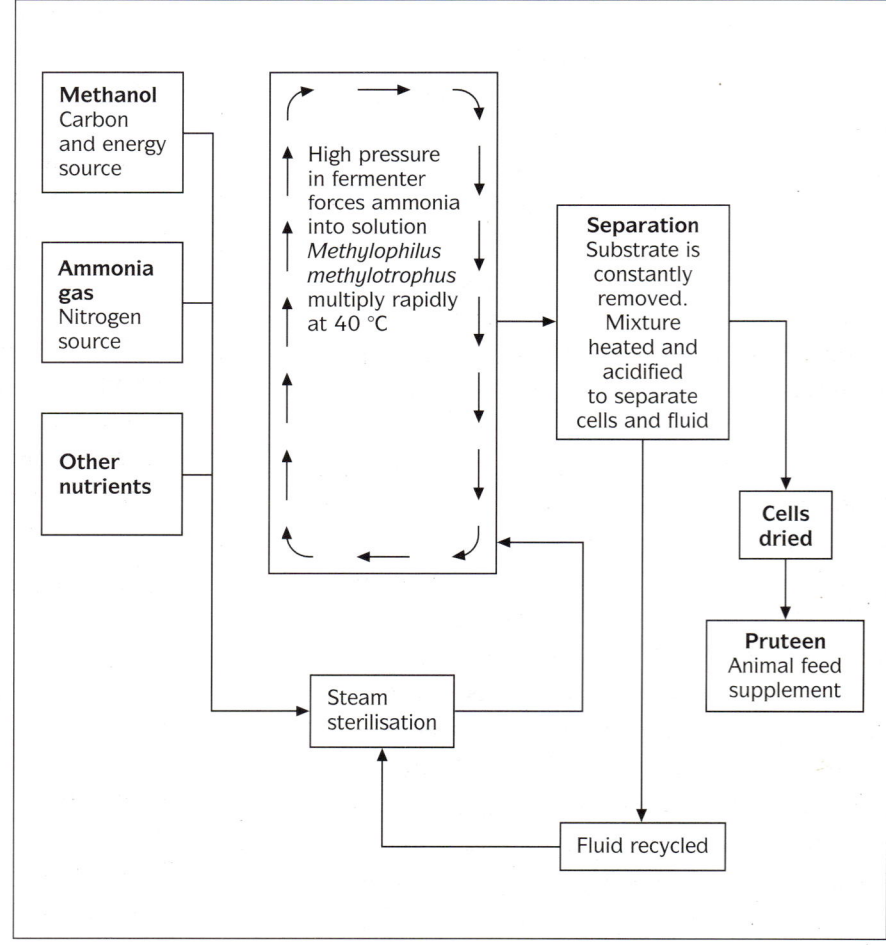

● *Figure 5.5* The manufacture of Pruteen, a single cell protein which was developed by ICI for use as a cattle feed.

SAQ 5.6
Why are widely available, cheap, waste products used as substrates for single cell protein production ?

SAQ 5.7
Why are microorganisms so suitable for SCP production?

SAQ 5.8
Continuous fermentation is not easy to achieve and currently batch processes are more popular in industry. Suggest why SCP production seems particularly suited to continuous production.

Yeast extract production

Breweries produce large amounts of yeast, and while some of it is used to inoculate the next brew, not all is required. Some of the yeast is filtered off and sold to whisky distilleries. Malt whisky is made in a similar way to beer, by fermenting a mash made from malted barley. However, to produce the whisky the fermented malt is boiled and the whisky distilled off. This process kills all the yeast in the brew, so the distiller has no left-over yeast to inoculate the next brew and needs a steady supply of fresh brewers' yeast.

Dried yeast is a rich source of water-soluble vitamins, including all the B-complex vitamins. It is a particularly rich source of the vitamins riboflavin and niacin, and is often sold in tablet form.

Spent brewers' yeast is also used to make other foods. During the nineteenth century, the German chemist Liebig became interested in the use of waste brewery yeast. He knew it was nutritious, and studied the problem of converting it to a palatable food product. Eventually he realised that, if he left the yeast to undergo a period of self-digestion and then concentrated it, he could make a product suitable for human consumption. Self-digestion of the yeast is called **autolysis**, and in this process the enzymes present in the yeast cell itself are used to break down the proteins, nucleic acids, carbohydrates and so on. The process discovered by Liebig occurs naturally, but it happens more quickly when the yeast is heated to 50 °C and salt is added. It normally takes about a day for most of the proteins to be broken down into amino acids, then the mixture is filtered and concentrated into a thick paste. One type of yeast extract manufactured in this way is marketed as Marmite.

Large quantities of fresh yeast arrive daily at the Marmite factory, and are subjected to autolysis in large tanks and copper vats. The liquid cell contents, called the **autolysate**, are separated from the cell walls by centrifugation and filtration. The residual cell walls are used for animal feed. Water is evaporated from the liquid autolysate in vacuum condensers to give a suitable consistency. It is carefully examined in the laboratories, then blended and flavoured with vegetable extracts before being packed in sterilised glass containers.

Yeast hydrolysates are made by boiling the yeast with hydrochloric acid, which hydrolyses most of the proteins to amino acids. It is then neutralised with sodium hydroxide, filtered, and concentrated into a thick paste. The final product tastes salty because of the salt produced by neutralisation of the acid.

Both autolysates and hydrolysates have a meaty flavour and are used as additives to food products where a meaty flavour is required, such as in soups and sauces, frozen foods, stews, hamburgers, sausages, gravies and to flavour snack products such as potato crisps. The meaty flavour of yeast autolysates is probably due to the large number of amino acids and small peptides it contains, but its flavour enhancement properties are probably due to nucleotides.

Making yogurt

Yogurt has been made for thousands of years in eastern Europe and western Asia. Traditional yogurt was much thinner and more acidic than the yogurt now readily available in shops and supermarkets which has been developed to suit modern tastes.

Yogurt is made by fermenting milk with a carefully cultured mixture of microorganisms. Whole, semi-skimmed or skimmed milk may be used. Sugar and/or starch may be added for certain products. The milk must first be tested to check for contamination by pathogenic bacteria due to lack of hygiene during milking and for antibiotics that might have been used to treat infections in cows. Then it is processed and a starter culture of bacteria is added to begin the fermentation. Commercial yogurt is usually made from concentrated skimmed milk. The milk may have been homogenised to make the mixture smoother and thicker and to lessen the risk of separation during incubation and processing.

The milk is heated to between 85 °C and 95 °C for 15–30 minutes. This has several effects including killing most of the bacteria in the milk, making it easier for the starter microorganisms to establish themselves. In addition the milk whey proteins are denatured so they can interact with the milk protein casein to produce a thicker texture. Most of the dissolved air is removed, improving the conditions for growth of the microaerophilic organisms in the culture. The milk is then cooled to just below 45 °C, which is the optimum temperature for the growth of lactobacilli in the starter culture.

At this point the starter culture is added and the milk is incubated at 38–44 °C for 4 to 6 hours or at 32 °C for 12 hours. The starter culture consists of a mixture of *Lactobacillus bulgaricus* and *Streptococcus thermophilus* which grow in symbiosis, that is they produce conditions which encourage growth in the other species. Lactobacilli break down protein to release peptides, which encourage the growth of the streptococci. When growing vigorously, the streptococci produce methanoic acid which stimulates the growth of lactobacilli. At the end of the incubation period, the pH has fallen to around 4.4. During the incubation *Lactobacillus bulgaricus* also produces lactic acid. Both microorganisms produce ethanal which gives the yogurt its characteristic flavour. Fruit, nuts or flavours may be added to the finished yogurt, having first been sterilised to prevent contamination by yeasts and other bacteria. After incubation, the thickened yogurt is cooled to 4.5 °C and held at this temperature for packing. When packed the yogurt is stored at 2 °C. The bacteria remain alive but are inactive at this temperature.

Recently, so-called 'bio' yogurts have become very popular. These produce a creamier tasting, sweeter yogurt. The starter culture for bio yogurts contains *Streptococcus thermophilus* and *Lactobacillus bulgaricus* as before, but also contains *Lactobacillus acidophilus* and *Bifidobacterium bifidum*.

SAQ 5.9

How might milk become contaminated with antibiotics? Why must the milk used in yogurt manufacture be free from all traces of antibiotic?

SAQ 5.10

Why must the milk mixture be cooled before the starter culture is added?

SAQ 5.11

Why does the pH fall during the incubation?

SAQ 5.12

Why is it not necessary to kill the bacteria before eating the yogurt?

SAQ 5.13

The yogurt vats and pipework in the factory must be sterilised between each batch. Why is this necessary and how might it be done?

Wine making

Traditionally, wine has been made using wild yeasts found on the skins of the grapes. Different strains of yeast are often confined to certain geographical areas and each gives a particular aroma and flavour to the wine which is characteristic of that region. Today, most modern wineries have their own specific strain of yeast which has been carefully cultured and selected for its properties. This helps to ensure consistency and reduces the chances of contamination and souring of the wine.

The harvested grapes are crushed to form the **must**. Traditionally the grapes are not pre-treated but in some areas, such as California, sulphur dioxide is used to treat the must so that any natural yeasts present are killed.

Traditionally, the natural yeasts present on the grape skins are allowed to ferment the sugars in the must. A complex succession of yeasts develop in the must, dominated by the true wine yeast, *Saccharomyces cerevisiae* var. *ellipsoideus*. Sterilised musts need to be inoculated with this yeast. Fermentation takes several days. The must from both red and white wine grapes is white and results in a white wine. Red wines are fermented with the grape skins present. As the sugars are converted to ethanol and carbon dioxide, the ethanol dissolves the red pigments from the grape skins and gives a red wine. For white wine the skins are removed.

Many wines, especially red wines, undergo a spontaneous secondary fermentation during the first year, called the **malo-lactic fermentation**. This process converts malic acid, present in the grapes, into lactic acid and carbon dioxide, reducing the acidity of the wine. This fermentation is carried out by a variety of lactic acid bacteria, such as *Pediococcus*, *Leuconostoc* and *Lactobacillus*.

Sparkling wines (champagne types) undergo a second alcoholic fermentation. Sugar is added and the carbon dioxide produced carbonates the wine, making it bubbly. Sherries are fortified with alcohol to about 15% and exposed to air. This develops a heavy surface growth of certain yeasts which produce the characteristic sherry flavour. Some European sweet wines, for example French sauternes, have pre-fermentation microbial treatment. Before the grapes are picked, they are naturally infected with the fungus *Botrytis cinerea*. This infection causes water loss, increasing the sugar content. In addition malic acid is destroyed, so the grapes are less acid. The must from these grapes is very sweet and is fermented by glucophilic yeasts which rapidly ferment the glucose leaving residual fructose. This makes it a very sweet dessert wine.

SAQ 5.14
If yeasts are already present on the skin of the fruit used for wine-making, why should some wine makers sterilise the must and then inoculate with yeast?

SAQ 5.15
How would the colour of a rosé wine be produced?

SAQ 5.16
Explain why a mature wine will taste quite different from a new one.

Beer manufacture

Beer is made from malted barley. To malt the barley the grains are soaked in water for 2–3 days, drained and then incubated at 13–17 °C for 10 days. This causes the grain to germinate, producing amylase enzymes, which convert the stored starch to maltose. The temperature is then raised to 40–70 °C to stop germination by denaturing enzymes. Malting is often carried out by specialist maltsters and the malt sent to the brewery. There are different types of malt, depending on the roasting temperatures used, and these impart different colours and flavours to the brew. Generally, lager malts are roasted at a lower temperature than beer malts.

The roasted grains are cracked open by passing between rollers. The crushed malt is called **grist**. This is mixed with hot brewing water at 62–8 °C in a large vessel. The mash stands for about two hours to allow the sugars to be dissolved out of the malt. It then passes into another large vessel where sugary liquid called **wort** is drained off. The grain is sprayed with hot water to wash the sugars out of the grains, which act as a filter. The spent grain is left behind and sold for cattle fodder.

Hops are added to give the characteristic bitter flavour of beer. Traditional breweries add dried hops in 'leaf' form, but modern breweries use hops which have been pressed into pellets, which reduces their transport and storage costs. A small amount of sugar is also added. Large copper vats are used to boil the wort for several hours to concentrate it. The boiled wort is separated from the spent hops which are sold for hop manure. The wort is then passed through heat exchangers to cool it to a suitable temperature for fermentation.

Yeast is added to the cooled wort in the fermenting vessel. *Saccharomyces cerevisiae* is used for beer and *S. carlsbergensis* for lager. Traditionally, lager yeasts grow at the bottom of the vessel and are called 'bottom fermenters' whereas beer yeasts grow on the surface of the wort and are known as 'top fermenters'. The newer varieties of beer yeasts are bottom fermenters, enabling breweries to use the same type of fermenter for either process. Initially, there is a fairly high oxygen content in the wort, and breweries may even aerate the brew, encouraging the yeast to divide rapidly so as to increase the numbers present. After this, conditions become anaerobic and fermentation begins. The yeast converts the sugars to ethanol and carbon dioxide in 2–5 days after which the yeast is separated off. Some is used to inoculate the next batch and the rest is sold for products such as yeast extract (Marmite). Sometimes the carbon dioxide is collected and sold.

Traditional beers are stored in barrels and allowed to 'condition'. Modern beers are filtered, pasteurised, standardised (brought to a standard colour and flavour) and canned or bottled.

Recently, there have been developments to produce both wine and beer by continuous fermentation methods. In these processes, the yeast is kept in its exponential growth phase so that the product is made much more quickly. This process is particularly popular for making lager, which can be made in about four hours instead of several days. However, although this process is more economical, the flavour and alcohol content are reduced.

SAQ 5.17

What is the difference between a 'top-fermenting' and a 'bottom-fermenting' yeast?

SAQ 5.18

Explain why beer or wine produced by continuous fermentation would have a lower alcohol content than its traditionally produced equivalent.

Bread manufacture

In bread making, flour is made into a dough with warm water and yeast. Enzymes, mostly amylases from the original wheat grain, act on the starch in the flour to produce a mixture of sugars. A small quantity of sugar may be added to the recipe to start the process more quickly. Some bread flours contain fungal amylases to speed up the process. The sugars, mainly glucose and maltose, are fermented by the yeast *Saccharomyces cerevisiae*. The dough is left in a warm place to **prove**. During this process, respiration in the yeast cells produces carbon dioxide gas which makes the dough rise when bubbles of gas are caught in the elastic dough. Ethanol is also made, but this is driven off during the baking process. Proteolytic enzymes in the yeast change the texture of the flour. In the large-scale manufacture of bread, bakeries may add other ingredients such as raising agents, stabilisers, whiteners and flavourings. Genetic engineering has been used to improve certain yeast strains, so that they prove the dough at lower temperatures, or produce carbon dioxide more quickly.

SAQ 5.19

Bread is made using *Saccharomyces cerevisiae*, the same yeast that is used to make beer, but brewers and bakers generally use different strains of this yeast. Why is this?

Enzymes in fruit juice production

Fruits such as apples are pressed to release their juice. To keep costs down it is essential for producers of fruit juice and concentrates to increase their yields during the manufacturing process. Often cold-stored fruit is used to ensure year-round availability of the most popular fresh juice but this produces problems.

The apple fruit is made up of cells linked by middle lamellae which contain insoluble protopectin. The cell walls are largely made up of the polysaccharides cellulose and hemicellulose which keep the cells quite rigid. During storage, the protopectin becomes partially changed into soluble pectin by pectinolytic enzymes that are found naturally in apples. Soluble pectin has a high water-binding capacity which reduces the yield of juice during pressing. So stored fruit produces a lower yield of juice than fresh fruit.

To overcome these problems, a mixture of powerful enzymes is added to the fruit pulp during the crushing stage. Pectinase breaks up the pectin chains and therefore reduces its water-binding capacity; hemicellulase weakens the cell walls making it easier to extract the juice *(figure 5.6)*

Many different types of fruit juices are now readily available in shops and supermarkets and there is a huge demand for these products. Enzymes have been specifically designed for the citrus industry, with a blend of different enzymes such as pectinlyase, polygalacturonase and hemicellulase, all balanced to get increased sugar extraction, reduced viscosity, increased clarity and the maximum yields of juice. These enzymes must be active at the low pHs found in citrus extracts *(figure 5.7)*.

Pressing berry and stone fruit pulp is a delicate process used to preserve the colour and aroma of the fruit and to get a good yield from expensive

● *Figure 5.6* Apple pulp **a** before and **b** after treatment with enzymes.

● *Figure 5.7* The effects of pH and temperature on the activity of citrus enzymes.

raw material. The use of enzymes can help to overcome the problems associated with juice extraction, such as low yields and colour loss. The strong colours (tannins and anthocyanins) and highly acidic pH of red fruits mean that the enzymes have to be carefully selected to retain their activity and stability under such conditions.

Enzymes and meat tenderisation

Animal carcasses used for meat are usually kept in cold storage for 10–12 days after slaughter. During this time, the lysosomes within the cells burst open and release proteases, which bring about autolysis of the tissues. These enzymes catalyse the breakdown of fibrous proteins such as collagen and elastin which hold the connective tissue together. This process releases the bundles of muscle fibres and therefore increases the tenderness of the meat.

In some countries, but not yet in the UK, a protease may be injected into the bloodstream of cattle just before slaughter, or added just after slaughter. One such enzyme, known as **papain**, is extracted from the sap of the papaya plant, *Caryca papaya*. Papain is sold commercially for application to meat in the home prior to cooking. However, most meat is tenderised during the cooking process before the proteases are denatured at around 90 °C.

SAQ 5.20

What are the arguments for and against the injection of a protease into cattle immediately prior to slaughter?

SUMMARY

- Biotechnology has an important role in agriculture: microorganisms can be used as silage inoculants; crop plants may be genetically engineered to become resistant to diseases, insects or herbicides; farm animals may be genetically engineered to have desirable properties, or they may be treated with hormones to give increased productivity.

- Microorganisms can produce single cell protein from waste substrates, and then be used as a human or animal foodstuff.

- Yeast is used in the production of bread, wine and beer. By-products, such as spent brewers' yeast, can be used in products such as yeast extract.

- Yogurt is made from milk by the action of selected bacteria.

- Enzymes are used in many ways to enhance food production, for example in fruit juice production and meat tenderisation.

Questions

1 a What is single cell protein?
   b Name an organism used to produce single cell protein.
   c Describe a medium in which this organism could be grown.
   d List **three** advantages of producing single cell protein rather than conventional protein-rich foods.
   e List **two** disadvantages of using single cell protein.
   f Fungi can be used to make meat substitutes for human consumption, such as Quorn. What structural features of fungi make them particularly suitable for this purpose?
   g Suppose you were working for a company which has recently discovered a new microorganism which produces single cell protein. You have been given the task of marketing this product. Initial market research reports suggest that the public are unwilling to accept single cell protein. Suggest why this might be, and devise some strategies for overcoming these difficulties so that the product can be successfully marketed.

2 Write an essay on ways in which biotechnology might help to overcome the problem of world food shortage.

3 Look at some food packets in your house, such as crisps, soups, gravy powders and sauce mixes. See if they use yeast hydrolysates or autolysates.

Chapter six

Biotechnology in health care and medicine

By the end of this chapter you should be able to:

1 describe and explain the application of genetic engineering in the production of insulin and growth hormone;

2 define and explain the term biosensor and explain why biosensors will be important in medical and related disciplines in the future.

Many **human proteins** can now be produced in culture, by introducing the necessary gene into the DNA of a yeast or bacterium. Among human proteins being made in this way are interleukins and interferon, both of which have an effect on the immune system. Interferon is made by virus-infected cells and protects other cells from becoming infected by viruses. Interleukins and interferon have potential benefits in cancer therapy.

Human growth hormone is a protein that is produced by the pituitary gland and regulates normal growth. Some children suffer from dwarfism because they lack this hormone and are unable to grow properly unless treated with it. Until recombinant human growth hormone was available the hormone was extracted from pituitary glands obtained from human corpses. However, the hormone produced this way was linked to the transmission of Creutzfeld–Jacob disease, which is caused by an infectious protein that slowly causes irreversible degeneration of the brain. This source of growth hormone has therefore been withdrawn. Using genetic engineering techniques the gene for human growth hormone has been inserted into bacterial cells so that growth hormone can be produced on a large scale. The hormone is used to treat children suffering from dwarfism, and in the US for those who are short in stature for other reasons. It is also being consid-

ered for use in treating the loss of protein and wasting that follows severe disease and injury.

While this technique was being developed, it was discovered that most people who needed treatment with growth hormone did not actually lack growth hormone itself, but another protein called growth hormone releasing factor (GRF). In normal people, GRF is produced in tiny amounts by the hypothalamus, and causes growth hormone to be released from the pituitary gland. Recombinant GRF can also be produced by genetic engineering and is now regarded as the best way to treat most growth deficiencies.

Scientists have also found that they can produce mice that are twice the normal size by giving them a gene for growth hormone. The gene can be inserted into a mouse embryo which is then implanted into a host mother. Offspring from the host mother will carry the new gene. Scientists are now trying to repeat this with farm animals in the hope of improving meat and milk yields.

● *Figure 6.1* Granules of human insulin forming inside genetically engineered *E. coli*.

plasmid

bacterium   bacterial DNA

Plasmid extracted and cut with restriction enzyme

cut plasmid

Human insulin extracted from pancreas cells

Amino acid sequence known, converted to triplet codes

Length of DNA synthesised which acts as human insulin-producing gene

human insulin-producing gene

Bacterial plasmid with human insulin-producing gene inserted

Plasmid re-introduced into bacterium to form recombinant

Genetically engineered recombinant bacteria multiply in fermentation tank and produce human insulin

fermentation tank

human insulin

injected into patient

● **Figure 6.2** Flow chart for the manufacture of human insulin using genetic engineering techniques.

A similar story has happened with the human protein **insulin** which is given to diabetics to control blood glucose level. The only source of insulin used to be from cattle and pig pancreases. This meant that supply of the hormone depended on a regular supply of pancreases from slaughtered animals. It also meant that some patients became allergic to the hormone because their bodies recognised it as a non-human protein and mounted an immune response. Genetically engineered human insulin is now being produced on a large scale, by inserting the human gene sequence into a bacterium *(figure 6.2)*. This has the advantage that the engineered product closely resembles human insulin and produces fewer side-effects than the insulin prepared from animal pancreatic extracts.

Other diseases which result from deficiencies of particular proteins may also benefit from developments in recombinant DNA techniques. Haemophilia is a hereditary disease in which the blood fails to clot properly. Most haemophiliacs lack a protein called **factor VIII**, and to prevent bleeding had to be treated with factor VIII obtained from human blood. Unfortunately, many haemophiliacs have developed AIDS because they received factor VIII obtained from infected blood. Although blood donated by donors can now be screened for HIV, many haemophiliacs feel much safer receiving the genetically engineered product.

Erythropoietin is another genetically engineered product which is helping many people. This hormone is produced by healthy kidneys and stimulates red blood cell production (erythropoiesis) in the bone marrow. Many patients with kidney failure do not produce enough erythropoietin from their damaged kidneys, which leads to anaemia (lack of red blood cells). Some of these patients have red blood cell levels which are 50% lower than in normal people, which means they suffer debilitating weakness and tiredness. Previously the only treatment was regular blood transfusions. The gene for erythropoietin has now been cloned, and inserted into Chinese hamster ovary cells. These cells are easy to grow in culture and several copies of the gene have been inserted, making them highly productive. The cells are grown in large fermenters, and the erythropoietin extracted from the culture medium has greatly improved the quality of life for kidney patients.

Biosensors

In order to survive, living things must be able to respond to changes in the environment, to detect food or to avoid toxic chemicals. Biological sensory systems can be extremely sensitive. 'Sniffer' dogs are able to detect the trail of humans, illegal drugs or explosives, while sharks can detect small amounts of blood from hundreds of metres away.

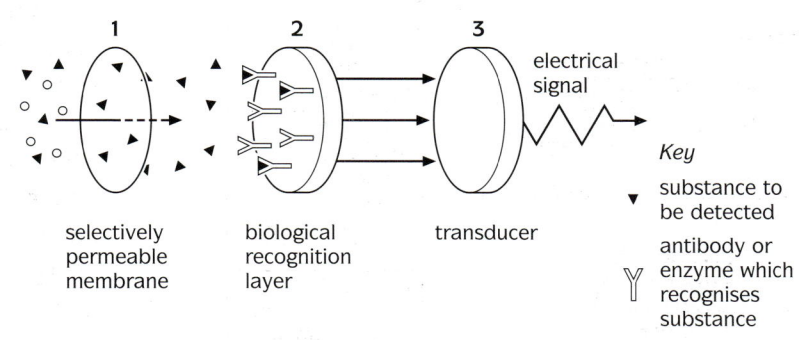

1 The substance to be detected passes through the membrane.

2 The substance binds to the recognition layer which may contain antibodies or enzymes; a reaction takes place.

3 The product of the reaction passes to a transducer and thus produces an electrical signal.

● *Figure 6.3* The parts of a biosensor.

In a biosensor there is a **biological recognition layer,** which may be an enzyme or enzymes, an antibody, a membrane component, an organelle, a prokaryotic or eukaryotic cell, or even living tissues. This layer is used to recognise a particular substance by producing a biochemical signal. The biological component is the part which ensures sensitivity and is responsible for the high degree of specificity shown by biosensors. The basis of the sensor is that, when two biological molecules interact, there are measurable physical or chemical changes, which can be measured by a transducer. The biological component is immobilised on to the surface of the transducer so that these changes can be measured accurately *(figure 6.3)*.

The **transducer** is an electrical device which can measure and amplify the signals from the biological reaction. Most transducers fall into two categories, potentiometric electrodes, which do not have any voltage applied, and amperometric electrodes, which have a constant applied voltage. Both types measure the voltage produced by the physical or chemical reaction. A familiar type of potentiometric electrode is the standard pH electrode. An enzyme can be immobilised and placed over the pH electrode, which specifically measures substrates or products as they are broken down or produced on the electrode surface. An example of an amperometric electrode is the oxygen concentration electrode. However, some biosensors are being developed in which the immobilised enzyme is close to a thermistor (temperature sensor), and the heat evolved during the biological reaction is measured. Clearly these can only be used when the external temperature is constant.

The first attempt to make a biosensor was in the 1960s when a sensor was developed which allowed surgeons to monitor blood glucose levels continuously during surgery. In this sensor the enzyme glucose oxidase was used. This catalyses the reaction between glucose and oxygen in solution to form gluconic acid and hydrogen peroxide. The enzyme was associated with a platinum oxygen electrode which measured the changing oxygen concentration as blood glucose levels changed.

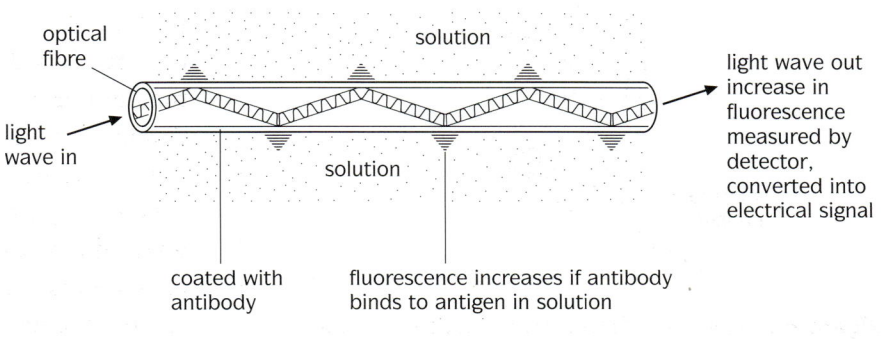

● *Figure 6.4* Optical fibre biosensor.

Optical fibre biosensors

A different approach involves the use of optical fibre technology. Antibodies can be tagged with fluorescent molecules and deposited on the surface of an optical fibre. When light travels along the fibre it is reflected back off the outer layer as shown in *figure 6.4*.

At the points of internal reflection, some of the light energy is transmitted outwards and when it meets the antibody layer some of it is deflected back into the fibre as fluorescence. The fluorescence increases when the antibody binds with its antigen. The intensity of light resulting can be detected by a sensor and converted into an electrical signal. This enables the presence of antigens to be detected in a sample of body fluid. Alternatively, the optical fibre can be coated with antigen and used to detect the presence of antibody. In the future, it should be possible to obtain an immediate indication of the presence of antibodies such as those produced in response to the HIV virus.

Microchip biosensors

Recently biosensors have been developed where the transducer is a microchip. One example is a biosensor, which is smaller than a ballpoint pen, that has been developed to detect the level of glucose in blood. The enzyme glucose oxidase is incorporated into a disposable probe which clips into the electrical device and the tip of the probe is dipped into a drop of blood. Glucose oxidase reacts with glucose in the sample to produce gluconic acid which generates an electric current in the chip. The current is relative to the amount of glucose present. It can also give warning of low blood glucose levels (hypoglycaemia). This makes it easier for a diabetic to calculate the dose of insulin needed. Similar sensors for alcohol and cholesterol are being developed.

Further development has produced probes where the enzyme is immobilised on the surface of a silicon chip making a **biochip**. Such biosensors are very tiny, some 2 mm across, and again one has been developed to detect blood glucose level.

When a positive charge forms on the surface of the chip, due to the gluconic acid produced, electrons flow to produce a signal which can be processed. As biochips are small and self-contained they are not easily damaged and can also respond to and process the signal. They can also be used continuously so it may soon be possible to implant a small glucose biosensor under the skin. This could control the release of insulin into the bloodstream automatically and act as an 'artificial pancreas'.

SAQ 6.1

Explain how a biosensor might be used to control insulin release in a person with diabetes.

SAQ 6.2

Design, in outline only, a biosensor which might be used to monitor cholesterol or alcohol levels in human blood.

Other uses of biosensors

Food, such as meat, may look fit to eat but may have been kept for too long in unsuitable conditions and may contain too many potentially harmful microorganisms such as *Salmonella*. Until recently, there was no immediate test of food freshness as the culture and identification of contaminating microorganisms generally takes several days. Now, however, a biosensor probe has been developed to detect the numbers of microorganisms in meat for use in the food industry. It consists of a sharp metal probe containing a biosensor which can be inserted into the meat. The biosensor measures the overall concentration of a range of different sugars in the meat. There is a correlation between sugar concentration and the number of microorganisms which feed on the meat. If the reading is above a certain level, then the meat is declared unsafe for human consumption.

This technique has many future applications and may be used to test the freshness of a wide range of food products. It has the advantage of giving an immediate result, vital in today's 'fast food' industry. It should soon be available for use in food preparation areas and supermarkets and should lead to a higher level of food safety.

Another use for biosensors could be to monitor processes in fermentation such as the build-up of waste products, changes in pH and availability of nutrients. These could be done with great accuracy and assist with feedback control.

Biochips can also be used to monitor changes in the environment. For example microorganisms that react with heavy metals and organic toxins could be used in the biochips. It may soon be possible to produce a range of biosensors, each incorporating a different microorganism, in order to monitor drinking water, or detect toxic gases, drugs or explosives. These would be very useful in pollution control and forensic science.

A Japanese company is manufacturing toilets which incorporate biosensors to measure glucose levels. When the patient urinates, a small amount of urine is trapped in a section of the toilet bowl and is directed into a chamber containing a glucose biosensor. The biosensor contains glucose oxidase which oxidises any glucose in the urine. The fall in dissolved oxygen is detected by an electrode. It is not yet possible to make a re-usable biosensor which is also reliable, so cheap, disposable biosensors are used. Nevertheless, each test will be much cheaper than hospital tests. Initially the toilets will be used in such places as geriatric day-care centres, but they have the potential for general health screening. In the future it may be possible to incorporate a multiple biosensor to monitor simultaneously glucose, lactate (an indicator of stress), urea and uric acid (indicators of kidney disease), haemoglobin (which indicates bleeding), antibodies (indicating infections or cancer) and protein concentration (which indicates the functioning of the digestive system). It might also be possible to monitor substances in faeces and sweat. A prototype skin biosensor, which resembles a watch, could be used to monitor fatigue and blood alcohol levels in lorry, bus and taxi drivers.

SUMMARY

■ Many human proteins can be produced in culture by inserting the necessary gene into the DNA of a bacterial or yeast cell. Recombinant human growth hormone is used to treat children suffering from dwarfism. Other useful proteins made in this way are human insulin, factor VIII for treating haemophilia, and erythropoietin which stimulates red blood cell production.

■ Biosensors are sensors that contain a biological component, such as an antibody or enzyme. These can be used to monitor such things as blood glucose levels and the progress of a fermentation. There are many potential uses of biosensors, for example in monitoring water quality, and detecting toxins, drugs and explosives.

Questions

1 Imagine that you are a scientist working for a company that makes biosensors. Make a three-dimensional model of a biosensor which could be used to explain the technique to a customer with very little scientific knowledge.

2 In the future, it might be possible for large employers to incorporate multiple biosensors in the company's toilets, to monitor such things as stress levels, general health indicators, alcohol and drug consumption, and so on. Would you welcome this, as a way of improving people's health, or would it be an infringement of personal freedom? Discuss.

Chapter seven

Biotechnology in manufacturing industry

By the end this chapter you should be able to:

1 define the term enzyme;

2 discuss the potential importance of enzymes as industrial catalysts;

3 explain the applications of the use of immobilised enzymes in manufacturing industries;

4 describe the use of enzymes in washing powders;

5 discuss the uses and production of biogas and gasohol by named microorganisms;

6 describe the use of microorganisms in mining and oil recovery.

Enzymes are biological catalysts, that is they accelerate the rate of chemical reactions. Enzymes are proteins and, in general, very specific, only catalysing one type of reaction and working on only one type of substrate. Substrates are converted to products through the formation of an intermediate enzyme–substrate complex. Many different enzymes are produced by living organisms and, in the field of biotechnology, microorganisms are now proving to be a readily available source of enzymes.

Without knowing it, humans have used enzymes for thousands of years, for making bread, beer, wine and cheese. At the start of this century, they were used commercially by Dr Otto Rohm who was trying to develop an improved method of softening hides and removing hairs before tanning. At the time, pigeon droppings and even dog faeces were used. Rohm found that the active components in these excreta were proteases, enzymes that digest proteins. He found that extracts from animal organs were successful and began to use enzymic extracts from pig and cattle pancreas, a less smelly alternative.

SAQ 7.1

Suggest some other enzymes which would be present in the animal excreta used in the tanning industry.

The development of microbial enzyme technology is comparatively recent. Now there is large-scale production of enzymes from microorganisms to catalyse a range of reactions at lower temperatures and pressures than would otherwise be required.

Since enzymes are proteins, they may be denatured by extremes of temperature and pH. However, industrial enzymes must be very robust and able to withstand a wide range of working conditions. For example they must be able to tolerate a wide temperature range, 10–55 °C, with an optimum around 40 °C. They must also have a wide pH tolerance as they may need to work in the presence of chemicals, such as sulphur dioxide, which usually inhibit enzyme action. Therefore the organisms grown for their enzymes must be selected carefully for these qualities. Indeed, some enzymes have exceptional properties, such as α-amylase which can degrade starch at over 100 °C.

Microorganisms have been found to be a valuable source of enzymes, for several reasons:

- they produce more enzyme molecules in relation to their body mass than most other organisms;
- they are easy to manipulate genetically and can be subjected to gene transfer techniques;
- product yield can be increased by means of strain selection, mutation and by optimising growth conditions;
- microorganisms are not influenced by climate and can be grown in suitable laboratories anywhere: this ensures independence of supply from world markets which may be subject to political influence;
- microorganisms can occupy a great variety of habitats and extremes of conditions, so their enzymes show an enormous range of pH and temperature characteristics.

Industry	Enzyme	Use	Difficulties
Dairy industry	animal-derived rennin	cheese manufacture	rennin can only be taken from very young animals, as rennin production decreases with age
	microbial rennin	increasingly used as a substitute for animal rennin	
	lipases	ripening in blue cheeses by extracellular lipases from mould, e.g. *Penicillium roquefortii*	
Brewing industry	amylase and protease enzymes in barley grain	break down starch and proteins in barley grains to sugars and amino acids during malting and mashing stages	
	industrially produced amylase, protease, glucanase	break down proteins and polysaccharides in the malt in some breweries	
	betaglucanase	breaks down yeast cell walls reducing cloudiness of beer	
	protease	breaks down yeast and improves clarity of beer	
	amyloglucosidase	breaks down sugars in production of low-calorie beer	
Baking industry	proteases	lowers protein content of flour for biscuit production	
	α–amylase enzymes from yeast	break down starch in flour to sugars which can be used by yeast	
Biological washing powders	mostly bacterial extracellular proteases	remove organic stains from washing	factory workers may become allergic; encapsulation of enzymes overcomes this
	amylases	mainly used in dishwasher detergent for removing starch residues	
Confectionery industry	α-amylases from *Bacillus subtilis*	produce glucose syrup as a sweetener from waste potato starch; α-amylases break down starch to short glucose chains (dextrins)	
	α-amylases from *Aspergillus niger*	hydrolyse dextrins to glucose: enzymes are immobilised and production is continuous; enzymes function for three months and have replaced the older acid hydrolysis method	

● *Table 7.1* Industrial applications of enzyme technology (continued on page 78)

Industry	Enzyme	Use	Difficulties
Agriculture Forestry	ligninases from *Sporotrichum pulverulentum*	most wood waste is not very useful as it contains lignocellulose and few organisms can utilise this: ligninases make cellulose available for animal feed or as an industrial substrate	
Textile industry	bacterial amylases	remove starch size, which is used to make fibres smoother, from threads during weaving; these enzymes withstand working temperatures above boiling point	
Leather industry	microbial trypsin	remove hair and excess tissue from hides and skin to make leather more pliable (trypsin used to be obtained from dung so microbial trypsin is preferred)	
Medical uses	trypsin	dissolve blood clots and clean wounds	
	various enzymes	laboratory diagnosis	

● **Table 7.1** (cont.)

Isolated enzymes

Traditional enzyme technologies, such as beer and cheese manufacture, use the whole microorganism. However, recent developments use isolated enzymes. This has several advantages:

■ when whole organisms are used, some of the substrate is converted to microbial biomass: using isolated enzymes is far less wasteful;

■ only one chemical process needs to be considered, so it is much easier to set up the optimum environmental conditions for that process;

■ only one enzyme is present, so there will not be wasteful side reactions;

■ it is easier to isolate and purify the desired product.

Most industrial enzymes are extracellular enzymes, that is those which are secreted by the microorganism into its substrate. These enzymes can easily be extracted from the contents of the fermenter. If intracellular enzymes are required, recovery is more complex, since the cells must be disrupted and the desired enzyme extracted from a mixture of many enzymes.

Industrial production of enzymes

Industrial microbiologists have many factors to consider when selecting microorganisms for enzyme production as shown in *figure 7.1*.

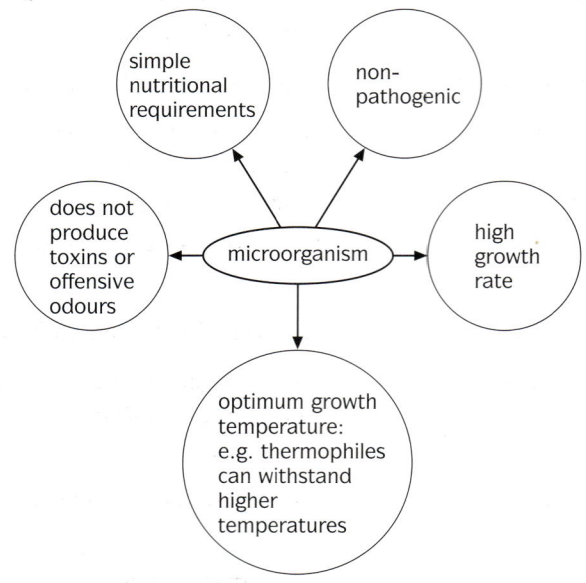

● **Figure 7.1** Factors to consider when selecting microorganisms for enzyme production.

● **Figure 7.2** Extraction of extracellular enzymes

Enzyme	Use(s)	Microorganism
α-amylase	breakdown of starch to maltose and dextrins, removing stains from clothes, flour improver, desizing starch on textiles, formation of glucose syrups	*Bacillus subtilis* *Aspergillus oryzae* *Bacillus licheniformis*
β-glucanase	prevents pipe blockage in brewing process by degrading β-glucan in beer, improves clarity of beer	*Aspergillus oryzae* *Bacillus subtilis*
catalase	preservative in drinks	*Aspergillus niger*
cellulase	washing powder, fabric improver and brightener, animal feed production from wastes such as straw	*Penicillium* spp. *Aspergillus* spp.
glucose isomerase	converts glucose to fructose, soft centres in chocolates, soft icing for cakes	*Streptomyces* spp. *Bacillus coagulans*
glucose oxidase	in biosensors to detect glucose in blood of diabetics	*Aspergillus niger*
lactase	conversion of whey to sweeter foods for people who are lactose-intolerant, in sweetened milk drinks, converting lactose to glucose and galactose	*Kluyveromyces lactis*
lipases	in washing powders to digest greasy stains, in cheeses to soften them	*Aspergillus oryzae* (genetically engineered)
pectinase	to extract juice from fruit pulp; to clarify wine and fruit juice	*Erwinia* spp.
protease	bating leather to make it soft and pliable, making meat extracts, in biological washing powders to clean protein stains like egg and blood	*Bacillus subtillis*
rennin	baby food manufacture, clotting milk in cheese making	*Kluyveromyces lactis* *Mucor* spp.
sucrase (invertase)	sweet manufacture	*Saccharomyces* spp.
streptokinase	treating bruises and blood clots	*Streptomyces* spp.

● **Table 7.2** Some enzymes produced by microorganisms

When the organism has been selected, genetic engineering may be used to produce a strain which gives a high enzyme yield with other useful properties such as stability. Any less favourable characteristics, such as odour, can be selected against.

Substrates for industrial enzyme technology should be cheap, plentiful and non-toxic. Commonly used substrates include whey, molasses, and waste starch from flour milling.

SAQ 7.2

What nutrients might be present in the substrates listed above?

SAQ 7.3

Suggest other substrates which might be suitable for industrial enzyme technology.

Enzymes are usually produced by batch fermentation, although it is sometimes found that better yields are obtained if different substances are added at various times during the fermentation in a fed-batch process.

There are several stages involved in the extraction of extracellular enzymes from the contents of the fermenter (*figure 7.2*):

■ filtering off the microorganism;
■ concentrating the enzyme by reducing the water content of the liquor which is often done by reverse osmosis;
■ removal of bacteria by filtration and addition of antibacterial agents to prevent contamination;
■ quality control, to ensure uniformity of the product;
■ packaging.

Immobilised enzymes

Recently, methods have been developed where enzymes are attached to insoluble materials that act as a support for the enzyme. The enzymes can then be held in place during the reaction, removed afterwards and used again. This is called **immobilisation** of the enzyme. Sometimes entire microbial cells are immobilised.

Immobilised whole cells are useful because, as it is not necessary to start with a pure enzyme the process is cheaper and quicker. Whole cells are immobilised in the same way as purified enzymes. They are being used increasingly for complex fermentations, such as waste treatment, nitrogen fixation, synthesis of steroids, semi-synthetic antibiotics and other medical products.

There are various methods for immobilising enzymes. They can be:

■ adsorbed on to an insoluble matrix, such as collagen (*figure 7.3a*);
■ held inside a gel, such as silica gel (*figure 7.3b*);
■ held within a semi-permeable membrane (*figure 7.3c*);

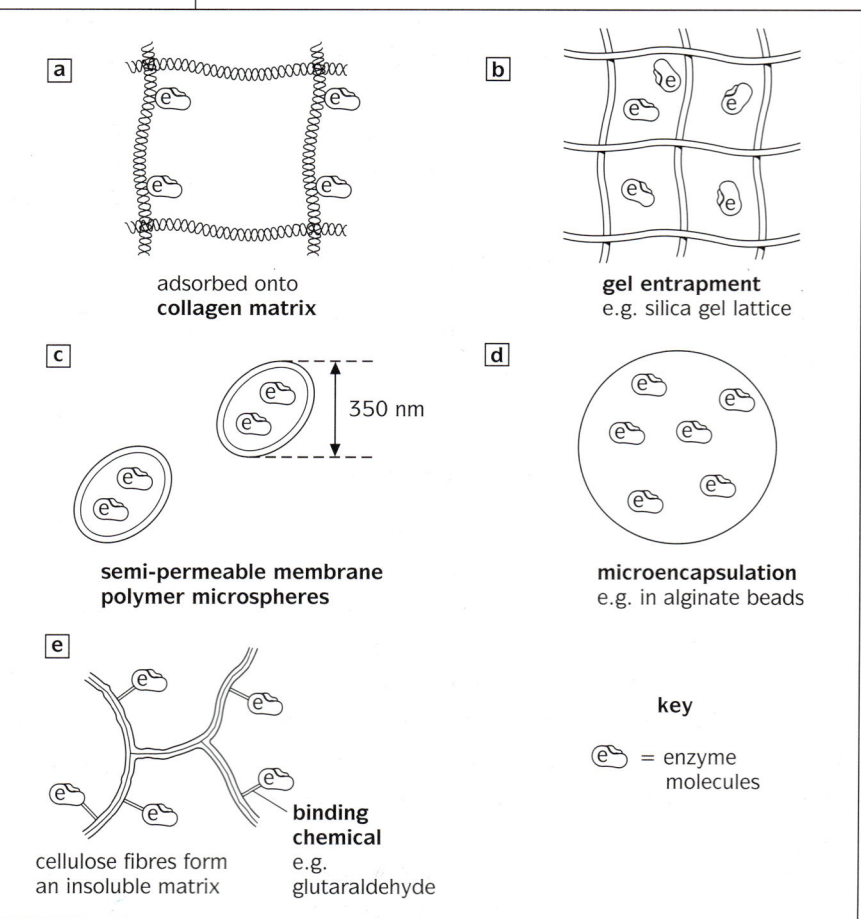

● **Figure 7.3** Immobilisation of enzymes.

■ trapped in a microcapsule, such as polyacrylamide or alginate beads (*figure 7.3d*). These processes all involve a physical bonding of the enzyme. They are not easy to carry out and generally result in low enzyme activity.

Alternatively, enzymes can be chemically bonded to the support medium (*figure 7.3e*). Since the enzymes are covalently bonded, enzyme activity is high, although preparing enzymes in this way is difficult.

The advantages of using immobilised enzymes are:

■ enzymes can be recovered and used over and over again, which is particularly useful when the enzyme is expensive or difficult to produce;

■ the product will not be contaminated by the enzyme, because the enzyme is held in a matrix;

■ the matrix protects the enzyme with a physical barrier, so that it is more stable at extremes of temperature and pH;

■ these properties make immobilised enzymes very suitable for continuous fermentations;

■ immobilised enzymes can be controlled more accurately;

■ immobilised whole cells mean that several enzymes can participate in the process simultaneously.

Immobilised enzyme technology is still developing rapidly and there are likely to be many new applications for immobilised enzymes in industry, medicine and waste disposal.

Enzymes in washing powders

In 1913 Dr Otto Rohm obtained a German patent for the use of extracts of pancreas to clean dirty clothes and his company started to manufacture the world's first enzyme detergent. The product consisted mostly of a mixture of washing soda (sodium carbonate) and pancreatic extract but was not a success. The soda made the pH of the solution very alkaline, thus reducing the activity of the enzymes.

During the Second World War there was a severe shortage of soap in Europe and further developments were made by Dr E. Jagg in Switzerland. However, progress was limited by a shortage of animal pancreases since they were reserved for the manufacture of insulin for diabetics. So it was after the war, in 1947, that products were made containing pancreatic trypsin with bile salts to aid emulsification.

Enzymes from bacteria

After the war fermenters were developed for the large-scale manufacture of penicillin. This technology was applied to the culture of other microorganisms and consequently, microbial enzymes. In 1959 a stain-removing product for clothes was launched in Switzerland containing bacterial protease with an optimum pH of around 7 (neutral). It worked better than the pancreatic extracts but was still unstable at the pH of the detergent (pH 9–10). In Denmark, Novo Industries produced a protease from *Bacillus licheniformis* that was active and stable in alkaline washing conditions. In 1963, Biotex was launched and was highly successful as a pre-washer and soaker. Soon the major detergent manufacturers began to introduce enzymes into their powders and today, enzymatic detergents account for 85% of the market in Western Europe. Biological washing powders now account for 25% of the enzymes sold worldwide.

SAQ 7.4

Biological washing powder manufacturers claim that their products 'remove biological stains'. What do they mean by 'biological stains'?

Safety of biological washing products

Unfavourable publicity in the early 1970s led to a marked fall in the use of biological washing powders. This arose when workers in the USA developed allergic reactions to the enzymes during manufacture. This problem was overcome by encapsulating the enzymes to make them dust-free, and greater emphasis was placed on the safe handling of enzymes during detergent manufacture. Since then the use of biological washing powders and, more recently, liquids has increased steadily, largely because they are so effective in removing dirt and stains at low temperatures.

Western Europe is the only region of the world where, by tradition, a hot wash is considered essential for cleaning clothes. This accounts for more than 25% of domestic electricity consumption. Most washing machines in the USA and Japan, for example, have a cold water fill and operate at lower temperatures for a longer cycle.

Since proteases currently in use work best at around 55 °C, the search is on for new enzymes with an optimum temperature around 20–30 °C. It may be possible to transfer genes from less productive microorganisms with suitable low temperature enzymes into more productive species by genetic engineering.

Using a variety of enzymes

Proteases will remove most protein-based stains, such as egg and blood, at low temperatures of 30–50 °C. However, without appropriate enzymes more difficult stains such as starches and grease need much higher temperatures to shift them. Amylases and lipases are therefore potentially very useful.

In 1989 amylase was added to Biotex to make it more effective over a wider range of stains. Care had to be taken to ensure that the new enzyme, a protein, was not digested by the protease already in the product. It is becoming important to consider the compatibility of all the ingredients used in the washing procedure, particularly with liquid detergents where the enzymes are in solution in the liquid and so are always active.

Very recently, detergent enzymes have been developed to remove fatty stains from fabrics at low temperatures. It was difficult to find a microorganism which produced high enough yields of lipase to make manufacture economically viable. It was also difficult to find a lipase that was not digested by the proteases in the detergent and would work at an alkaline pH. A suitable lipase was found in a strain of the fungus *Humicola*, but the fungus was not sufficiently high yielding. Therefore the gene for the lipase was transferred by genetic engineering into *Aspergillus oryzae* which is more easily cultured in a fermenter and gives high yields of the enzyme.

● **Figure 7.4** Cotton fibres **a** before and **b** after treatment with cellulase.

Whilst proteases, amylases and lipases all digest particular stains, a new kind of enzyme acts by restoring the fabric itself. Cellulase digests away any loose and damaged microfibrils from cotton fibres, restoring the original smooth surface. It also softens the fabric, which makes it an alternative to fabric conditioners, and removes dirt clinging to the cellulose microfibrils.

Enzymes offer an environmentally friendly alternative to the harsh solvents and high phosphate detergents otherwise required to shift dirt and stains. Very extensive tests have shown that there are no discernible harmful effects on the environment once enzymes are washed down the drains and into water courses. Because they are so effective at lower temperatures, they are also less demanding on valuable energy resources.

The production of methane

Methane is a gas which is produced naturally during the anaerobic decay of plant and animal material, such as in the cow's rumen stomach or below the surface of peat bogs. This gas can be used as a replacement for natural gas and research has been carried out to find ways to make it cheaply and economically. The rumen of ruminant animals, such as the cow, is a complex fermentation system with many different microorganisms involved. Attempts to set up similar processes in fermenters need precise monitoring, since it is not easy to imitate the natural process. However, methane production can be done on a very low technology scale, which is suitable for developing countries.

Sewage

Many sewage treatment plants now have anaerobic digesters for sewage treatment. The sludge is separated from the liquid effluent, which is treated aerobically. The semi-solid sludge is placed in digesters and warmed to 15 °C. Microorganisms naturally present in the sludge, such as *Methanobacterium*, *Methanococcus* and *Methanothrix*, digest the organic sludge and produce methane which can be used to power the sewage treatment plant.

Urban waste, landfill gas

In recent years in the UK a biofuels programme,

● **Figure 7.5** Biogas fermenter in Nepal.

with the backing of the Department of Energy, has concentrated on the production and use of gases formed when domestic refuse biodegrades in landfill sites. Refuse is decomposed under anaerobic conditions, using microorganisms such as *Methanobacterium* which are naturally present, to yield a mixture of gases containing large quantities of methane. One successful scheme is at Bidston Moss, Merseyside, UK.

Formerly a peat mossland, Bidston Moss has been used as a waste disposal site for over 50 years, receiving mostly domestic refuse since the mid 1980s. The waste has been tipped to form a mound about 20 m thick. Vertical wells were drilled to collect gas from an area covering about 40% of the site. The gas is transported, via pipelines, to a header pipe which circles the site. The gas flow and yield are controlled by a series of valves. The gas is dried before being piped 2.5 km along a polyethylene pipe, laid one metre underground, to a large factory complex where the gas is used to raise steam in a huge boiler. This site yields between 1–1.5 million therms of gas annually. At Bidston Moss, the scheme has proved to be economically viable due to the large volume of gas released and the convenient location nearby of a commercial customer. It has also helped to cut down on the unpleasant smells formerly released from the site. Other local authorities are liquefying landfill gas and using it to run their vehicles.

Biogas fermenters

These have been used for hundreds of years in some countries. In India, Pakistan and China, for example, systems range from very small family schemes to quite large biogas plants. Animal dung and water are allowed to ferment in almost anaerobic conditions, to produce **biogas**, a mixture of methane and carbon dioxide which is useful as a fuel. Any organic material may be used in these fermenters, for example human waste and crop residues such as straw. It is possible to grow crops specially as a substrate for methane production. In addition, the wastes from methane digesters can be useful by-products. The residue is rich in such nutrients as ammonia and phosphates, and can be used as a soil conditioner or even animal feed. As well as methane, other fuels such as propanol and butanol can be made this way. Utilising digester wastes for soil conditioning increases the cost-effectiveness. However, while this is a useful small-scale process, it is unlikely to be commercially viable on a large scale because:

■ methane can be produced far more cheaply from coal;
■ natural gas is cheaper than microbially produced methane;
■ there are many natural sources of methane;
■ gas is expensive to store, transport and distribute;
■ it is expensive and difficult to liquefy.

Some farms now place animal manure and other crop residues into anaerobic digestion tanks. Here, the waste is fermented by microorganisms and the methane produced is collected, liquefied and used to power farm machinery. In some cases it may be used to fire boilers, which heat glasshouses and produce early crops of tomatoes, peppers and other vegetables.

SAQ 7.5

Design a simple biogas fermenter which could safely be used by a family in a developing country.

SAQ 7.6

A semi-solid residue remains after biogas has been produced in a fermenter. Suggest a use for this residue.

Energy from biomass

The world has become increasingly dependent on non-renewable energy sources such as petrol. World oil supplies are predicted to run out in about 50 years and scientists are working to overcome the crisis by finding alternative, preferably renewable, energy sources. Microorganisms offer one solution to this problem.

Biomass is an attractive energy source, since it is formed by photosynthesis using energy from sunlight which is effectively unlimited. At present a great deal of biomass is wasted. Biomass includes straw, timber

and crop residues. Microorganisms can make use of these wastes and at the same time help to solve waste disposal problems. In addition, low-tech designs for fuel production are available, for use in developing countries or on a small scale, where traditional energy production methods are less effective.

Almost any organic waste materials can be used to produce fuel. This can be highly cost effective because such materials are cheap to obtain and using them saves the often high cost of disposal. It is also possible to grow crops specially for energy production on land unsuitable for growing food-stuffs or where the climate is suitable for rapid growth. Sugar cane is already being grown in Brazil for this purpose. In the UK, forestry is likely to be the most useful energy crop, and willow, grasses and new species of rapidly growing conifers are being developed for this purpose.

Gasohol production

Ethanol has been produced by fermentation for thousands of years and as long ago as 1890 it was used as a motor car fuel. In the 1920s and 1930s cars were run on ethanol in some parts of the world and also during the Second World War when there were fuel shortages. At present, most industrial alcohol is made synthetically, from by-products of the petrochemical industry. However, many developing countries have always used traditional fermentation methods to make industrial alcohol, since cheap raw materials are available. As the price of oil increases, this method will become more attractive to industrial countries. Since alcohol can be converted easily into ethene and other similar compounds, which are the basic raw materials in plastics manufacture, it could replace oil in this industry.

Brazil has made the greatest advances in the production of ethanol by traditional methods, and is currently the world leader in producing fuel alcohol, called **gasohol**. Gasohol is also produced in the USA. Many carbohydrate substrates are used, including sugar cane, cassava roots and cellulose waste. Cassava roots contain starch which must be hydrolysed first to sugars. Cellulose waste, such as timber and straw, needs quite complex pre-treatment with lignocellulase enzymes or chemicals.

In the USA, corn is the raw material in the production of fuel alcohol, with other useful by-products, e.g. corn oil, corn syrup, corn steep liquor and distiller's yeast

● *Figure 7.6* Ethanol production.

The sugar-rich substrate is placed in a fermenter and yeast is added. The yeast ferments the sugars to ethanol, which is obtained from the contents of the fermenter by distillation *(figure 7.6)*.

Brazil is building over 500 fermentation and distillation plants and eventually aims to supply the country's entire petrol needs with ethanol. At present, alcohol production is mainly by the traditional process but much research is taking place. It is hoped that more efficient genetically engineered microorganisms will be developed and that newer fermenter designs and immobilised enzyme technology will improve efficiency. Distillation costs can be reduced by using a cheap fuel. For example **bagasse**, the waste from sugar cane, has proved to be economical for raising steam for the process.

Using biomass as a fuel source could help solve another problem. The burning of fossil fuels releases carbon dioxide, which has been locked away for millions of years, into the atmosphere. It is thought that the increased amount of carbon dioxide in the atmosphere might increase the **greenhouse effect**, that is the trapping of infrared rays from the Sun within the atmosphere, and lead to an increase in temperature of the air. This could have many effects, such as changing world weather patterns and melting polar ice caps to raise sea levels. If biomass is used as an alternative, where the carbon dioxide has only recently been fixed in the plant tissue, there would be no net effect on the carbon dioxide levels in the atmosphere.

A range of microorganisms have been used in the production of ethanol, using many different carbohydrates as substrate. Traditionally ethanol production has relied on the use of yeasts, mostly *Saccharomyces* spp. In South America *Zygomonas mobilis* has been used for many years in the production of tequila, and in Indonesia and Africa to make palm wine. Recent research has shown that *Zygomonas* is more efficient than yeasts in converting sugar to ethanol. It also produces only trace amounts of glycerol, a major by-product in yeast fermentation, so that there is a higher ethanol yield. The smaller *Zygomonas* cells have a higher surface area to volume ratio and so take up sugar and give out ethanol more quickly than yeast. Its fermentation rate is faster than yeast and it has a greater ethanol tolerance limit.

A technique has been developed to produce ethanol using *Zygomonas* in continuous culture, rather than by the more traditional batch method. The cells are immobilised on to an inert support medium and packed into a column. The substrate, in solution, flows slowly past. This process seems to be very promising.

$$CuFeS_2 + 2Fe_2(SO_4)_3 + 2H_2O + 3O_2 \longrightarrow CuSO_4 + 5FeSO_4 + 2H_2SO_4 + \textbf{energy}$$
for growth

30 °C, pH 2

low grade ore heap

pumping station

leaching solution

$CuSO_4$ solution collection point containing scrap iron

action of iron on copper sulphate:
$$CuSO_4 + Fe \longrightarrow Cu + FeSO_4$$
metal   metal

● *Figure 7.7* Microbial mining.

At present ethanol is still more expensive than oil, but an increasing number of governments are funding research because of the environmental benefits, and because supplies of oil are limited so that the price of oil will eventually rise substantially.

Microbial mining

Some bacteria are useful in extracting metals from low-grade ores. This is because they are **chemo-autotrophic**, which means they derive their energy from inorganic chemicals. Bacteria of the genus *Thiobacillus* are used commercially to extract copper and uranium from otherwise uneconomic reserves. Cobalt, lead and nickel may also be extracted in this way in the near future. The extraction process may require extremes of environmental conditions, such as pH and temperature. Genetic engineering is being used to confer acid- and heat-resistance on these organisms.

Copper mining

In the 1700s Spanish miners knew that they could cause free copper to seep out of piles of copper ore simply by running water over it. What they did not realise was that the moisture allowed bacteria which were naturally present to oxidise the sulphur which was binding the copper in the ore. One of the bacteria responsible for this, *Thiobacillus ferrioxidans*, can oxidise insoluble chalcopyrites ore and convert it to the soluble salt copper sulphate. Sulphuric acid is produced during the process, yet the organism is able to flourish in these conditions. Copper can be extracted by reacting the copper ions with scrap iron. This method is responsible for about 25% of the copper produced in the USA.

Uranium mining

In uranium mining areas it has been found that water collects in underground pools which are a rich source of this radioactive element. This is because microorganisms naturally present on the rock face break down the low-grade uranium ore. This process can be enhanced by pumping the run-off water, containing bacteria such as *Thiobacillus ferrioxidans*, into the mine. The resulting water is pumped out and is rich in uranium ions. This makes extraction economical and reduces environmental damage.

Uranium and copper are not the only metals which can be mined using bacteria. In Brazilian, Australian and South African gold mines, micro-organisms are used to treat the raw ore before final processing with cyanide to extract the metal.

Bioaccumulation

Some microorganisms are able to accumulate metals, and this property can be exploited, both for extracting valuable metals from low-grade waste and for detoxifying wastes. Some bacteria, such as *Pseudomonas* spp. can accumulate metallic mercury. *Pseudomonas aeruginosa* accumulates uranium from effluents, while some *Thiobacillus* species accumulate silver.

Oil recovery and oil digestion

Oil recovery

Conventional oil extraction technology can only extract about 50% of the world's subterranean oil reserves. The rest is trapped in rock or is too viscous to pump. Microbial-enhanced oil recovery is a way of recovering more of this trapped oil by the application of microorganisms or their products. Biological compounds may be injected down wells where they can act in several ways. Firstly, surfactants are used to reduce surface tension and release trapped oil by making it more fluid. Emulsan is one such surfactant.

Emulsan is a polysaccharide polymer produced by microorganisms. It is very substrate-specific and acts only on certain hydrocarbons. Such polysaccharide polymers are found in the bacterial capsule, outside the microbial cell wall and membrane. They can be synthesised in batch culture and production is enhanced when there is an excess of carbon substrate in the growth medium.

A second approach is to add a viscosity enhancer, such as xanthan gum, to the water which is pumped down the well so that it is better at pushing oil out of crevices in the rock. *Xanthomonas* is the bacterium which produces xanthan gum and this can be done on a large scale using batch fermentation.

Dealing with oil pollution

There are some species of microorganisms which are able to feed on the hydrocarbons in oil. However, each species is only able to consume a very limited range of hydrocarbons. Several strains of the bacterium *Pseudomonas* occur naturally and can be used in a mixture to clear up oil-contaminated water. Genetic engineering techniques have enabled the production of a 'superbug' which has several 'oil-consuming' genes inserted into one organism. Plasmids containing genes for the degradation of naphthalene, xylene, camphor and octane have been combined into one strain of *Pseudomonas* which is still under trial in field conditions.

However, it is unlikely that bacteria could ever cope fully with a major oil pollution disaster, such as the deliberate release of crude oil into the Persian Gulf during the Gulf War. This is because the bacteria only work at the oil–water interface, not throughout the oil slick which can be quite thick. Also, the rate of bacterial activity depends on the ambient temperature, which can be quite low in parts of the world, such as Alaska which was the site of the Exxon Valdez oil tanker disaster.

There has been some concern about the release of such genetically engineered superbugs into the environment, as would be required if oil slicks were sprayed with a culture of bacteria. In the long term, it is possible to envisage the localised use of such sprays to clear oil from areas such as rock surfaces. The natural process of decay could certainly be enhanced in this way and provide a more environmentally friendly method than spraying with detergents which simply emulsify the oil but do not degrade it.

SUMMARY

■ Enzymes are biological catalysts and have been useful for many years in brewing, bread making, cheesemaking and tanning.

■ More recently, it has been found that microorganisms are a particularly good source of enzymes, which have been produced on a large scale. These specialist enzymes have been used in a variety of industries, and can also be immobilised so that they may be used repeatedly.

■ One particular use of enzymes is in the manufacture of biological washing powders.

■ Microorganisms may be used to assist in oil recovery, especially where conventional oil recovery is uneconomic, and in mining, to extract metal from low-grade ore and to detoxify wastes.

■ Microorganisms may also be used to produce biogas rich in methane, from waste products such as sewage, domestic refuse and agricultural residues. Ethanol may be made from crop residues and used as a fuel, for example in car engines. These could be important sources of energy in the future.

Questions

1 Why are microorganisms particularly suitable as a source material for enzyme production?

2 Construct a table, using the headings below, listing as many examples as possible:

Substrate	Microorganism	Enzyme	Use

3 Where could a scientist look for bacteria and fungi which might be a source of a useful enzyme? How would the scientist then attempt to increase enzyme production by the organism concerned?

4 Outline the main steps in the industrial preparation of a named enzyme.

5 The enzyme xylanase is now being used instead of chlorine to bleach paper. Suggest **two** advantages of using xylanase.

6 What advantages are there in using immobilised enzymes? Give **two** examples of their use.

7 Increasingly, immobilised whole microbial cells are being used as biocatalysts. Why is this an important production process?

8 You are working as a research biochemist for a large washing powder manufacturer trying to make a new product to help clean baby clothes. What enzymes might you include in the mix, bearing in mind the types of stains encountered and the properties of the enzymes?

9 What environmental and ecological benefits are there in tapping landfill sites for methane production?

Answers to self-assessment questions

Chapter 1

1.1 Plasmid = circular piece of DNA not joined to chromosome

mesosome = infolding of membrane, probably used in cell division

cell wall = the main component of this is the peptidoglycan murein

capsule = slimy layer surrounding some bacterial cell walls

pilus = made of pilin, used in conjugation in some species

1.2 Blue-greens are prokaryotic because they are approximately 2 μm in diameter, lack a true nucleus, have a naked coil of DNA, with a cell wall similar to that of Gram negative bacteria, 70S ribosomes, and pigments not in chloroplasts but incorporated into infoldings of the plasma membrane, called lamellae.

1.3 Blue-greens have a very primitive structure, are found ubiquitously in water and damp places, and are primary colonisers of bare ground. In the primitive atmosphere of Earth little free oxygen was available, so the earliest life-forms on Earth are thought to have been similar to the blue-green bacteria, that is, prokaryotic, photosynthetic organisms. Fossil remains of organisms resembling the blue-greens have been found dating from around three billion years ago.

1.4 Features shared by the four phyla of protozoa include:
cytoplasm which can exist in the two states, plasmasol and plasmagel; phagocytosis; contractile vacuoles; food vacuoles; reproduction by binary fission; gas exchange by diffusion across cell membrane; nitrogenous waste is ammonia.

Distinguishing features: Rhizopoda are able to move using pseudopodia; Zoomastigina move using flagella; Ciliophora have many cilia which are organelles of locomotion; Apicomplexa are parasitic and some have different forms during their life cycle in the human and the mosquito; Ciliophora have two types of nucleus.

1.5 **a** Ascomycota: septate hyphae, asexual reproduction by non-motile spores called conidia borne on conidiophores, sexual reproduction by fusion of the male conidium with the female ascogonium. Yeasts are also ascomycetes, differing from other fungi in being unicellular and having a cell wall composed largely of polymers of glucan and mannan.

b Basidiomycota: septate hyphae, asexual reproduction usually absent, sexual reproduction by fusion of hyphae of two compatibility groups resulting in fruiting body bearing basidiospores.

c Zygomycota: aseptate hyphae, asexual reproduction by non-motile spores within a sporangium borne on a sporangiophore, sexual reproduction by fusion of gametangia to form a zygospore.

1.6 **a** In common with higher plants: eukaryotic cell structure and a cell wall.

b Different from higher plants: cell wall is made of chitin, not cellulose; lack chlorophyll and do not photosynthesise; not composed of separate cells (even when hyphae are septate, there are usually several nuclei in each compartment).

1.7 *Hypha*: filament of a fungus, surrounded by chitinous cell wall and containing cytoplasm and organelles.

Mycelium: filaments of fungus forming an interwoven mass.

Septum: cross wall formed in hyphae of some fungi, dividing the cytoplasm into compartments.

Bud: a daughter yeast cell being formed from the parent cell.

Basidium: a cell in the fruiting body of basidiomycete fungi which bears basidiospores.

1.8 The lytic cycle brings about the sudden death or lysis of the host cell, whereas the lysogenic cycle does not destroy the host cell immediately. In the lytic cycle, the viral DNA causes the host cell to reproduce viruses, whereas the lysogenic cycle incorporates the viral nucleic acid into the host cell DNA so that it is passed on to each daughter cell every time the host cell divides.

1.9 Viruses contain nucleic acid like other living things, but have many non-living features. They do not have a cell structure; they can only reproduce themselves within other living cells; outside a cell they are rather like crystals; they have DNA or RNA but never both; they have no metabolism.

Chapter 2

2.1 a Complex – it contains meat extract, which is of unknown chemical composition.

b Meat extract and peptone.

c Meat extract and peptone (amino group in proteins).

d There will be some trace mineral ions in tap water which organisms may need for growth.

e To ensure the medium is at the correct pH for the organisms' enzymes. It also ensures that the medium is neutral, since microorganisms produce acids as they respire.

2.2 a (i) Potato dextrose agar is a complex medium, whereas Czapek–Dox agar is a synthetic medium.

(ii) Potato dextrose agar: glucose and potato are the main carbon sources. The nitrogen source will be nitrates and amino groups from proteins in the potato tissue. Mineral salts and other growth factors will be present in the potato tissue.
Czapek–Dox agar: sucrose is the carbon source, and sodium nitrate is the nitrogen source. The other ingredients are mineral salts.

b (i) Czapek–Dox agar is necessary here. You would need to modify the medium to make a number of variants, such as use potassium nitrate instead of sodium nitrate to find the effect of sodium ions on the growth of fungi.
(ii) If environmental factors only are being varied (such as light intensity, temperature, carbon dioxide levels) then either medium would do, provided the potato dextrose agar (PDA) was all made as one batch. If nutritional factors were included, only Czapek–Dox medium would be suitable, made up as suggested in (i).
(iii) Either medium would do, provided the PDA was all made with the same potatoes. It would then be dispensed into smaller amounts, each with a different buffer added.
(iv) Only Czapek–Dox medium is suitable, making it with different carbon sources, such as lactose or galactose instead of sucrose.
(v) Either medium would do, provided the PDA was all made with the same potatoes.

Czapek–Dox medium could be used for all the experiments listed, but where PDA can be used it may be preferable to do so as it is less time-consuming to make. On the other hand, Czapek–Dox medium is always the same, which means experiments could be repeated. PDA made on a subsequent occasion would be slightly different, due to variations in potatoes.

2.3 To allow the agar tablets to absorb water and dissolve properly.

2.4 If too much steam builds up, the safety valve may release all the pressure.

2.5 The McCartney bottles are removed from the autoclave, then placed on their sides with their lid end raised slightly. When the agar has solidified, the bottles can be stood upright.

2.6 Agar solidifies at 42 °C. An easy way to test for this is to hold the flask in the palm of the hand. Between 50 °C and 42 °C it can be held comfortably.

2.7 To destroy any microorganisms from the atmosphere which may be present there.

2.8 Flaming the neck of the flask; holding the bung in the hand and replacing it quickly; lifting the petri dish lid only a little, and holding it above the plate while pouring; not putting the petri dish lid down on the bench; working in the vicinity of a bunsen burner.

2.9 If agar is present on the lid, microorganisms will grow on it and obscure the view of the base. If it splashes between the lid and base, it is possible that microorganisms from the petri dish might grow on the agar and escape.

2.10 Plastic items like these would melt at the temperature of an autoclave.

2.11 The optical density is 52%. You could find the number of cells in a stated volume of this sample using a haemocytometer.

2.12 Student **A** used a haemocytometer, which gives a total cell count. Some of the cells this student counted were dead, but dead cells and live cells cannot be distinguished by appearance. Student **B** used pour plates, which involves incubating the cells and counting the colonies which develop. Colonies can only grow from living cells, so this method gives a viable count which will be lower.

2.13 *Obligate anaerobe*: these are microorganisms which can only grow in the absence of oxygen, such as *Clostridium botulinum*.
Facultative anaerobe: these are microorganisms which grow aerobically when oxygen is present, but can grow (less efficiently) when oxygen is absent, such as *E. coli*.
Mesophile: these are microorganisms which grow best at 20–40 °C, such as *E. coli*.
Psychrophile: these microorganisms grow best at temperatures below 20 °C, such as *Listeria monocytogenes*.

Chapter 3

3.1 Making yogurt and bread, treating sewage and producing methane from landfill sites are traditional biotechnology processes. This is because they all use microorganisms in manufacturing or service industries. Growing tomatoes and potato crisp manufacture are not necessarily biotechnology processes, but biotechnology may be involved in genetically engineering new strains, using plant tissue culture, or in making additives such as monosodium glutamate, to flavour the crisps.

3.2 Crop residues, such as straw, sugar cane, waste etc., could be put into a vessel, and *Clostridium acetobutylicum* added. The vessel needs to have a lid to maintain anaerobic conditions, and a vent for waste gases. *Clostridium* secretes amylases to convert starches to sugars, and then ferments the sugars to propanone and butanol. If there is a lot of cellulose in the crop residues, a suitable cellulose-digesting microorganism could be used for pre-treatment of the waste, or cellulase could be added.

3.3 Biotechnologists would try to block the pathway leading to product **D** if possible. They would probably try to do this by inhibiting one of the enzymes in that pathway, for example the enzyme converting **A** to **B**. This would ensure that most of substance **A** is converted to product **X**.

Another approach would be to develop a strain of the organism which is more efficient at producing **X**, maybe by using genetic engineering techniques.

3.4 GGCATGAATCTATTAGCGAAGCTTCCCGGGATCTACTGGAATTCGCCGAAGCTTTC
CCGTACTTAGATAATCGCTTCGAAGGGCCCTAGATGACCTTAAGCGGCTTCGAAAG

⋯⋯⋯ = Hind III restriction sites

– – – = Eco R1 restriction site

3.5 These microorganisms are able to survive at high temperatures, therefore their enzymes must have a high optimum temperature. This means they would be able to operate efficiently at high temperatures in an industrial fermenter. However, they would require the fermenter to be heated at the start of the fermentation

3.6 A patent is the exclusive right to manufacture or use an invention. Companies may not always obtain a patent because:

■ the invention may not be sufficiently different from other patented inventions so a patent may not be granted;

■ in filing a patent, companies must give a detailed description. They may feel this could give their competitors an advantage and so decide to keep the invention a trade secret instead.

3.7 It would be a gene which renders the organism unlikely to survive in a normal environment. For example, it might be a gene for a faulty enzyme so that the organism is unable to synthesise an essential amino acid. In the laboratory, this amino acid can be supplied in the medium, but in the external environment, the amino acid is unlikely to be found.

Chapter 4

4.1 This means that air from the laboratory does not directly mix with external air, and vice versa. If a microorganism were to contaminate the air in the laboratory, it would therefore be contained in the laboratory, and the spillage could be dealt with. It also avoids contaminating microorganisms from the external environment entering easily.

4.2 Bacteriophages readily infect their host bacteria and replicate rapidly, so any bacteriophage infection would quickly destroy the bacterial cells in an industrial fermenter.

4.3 a The footbath reduces the number of contaminating microorganisms being brought into the room on the soles of shoes. Since the fermenters have open tops, it would be possible for these organisms to enter the fermenters unless hygiene precautions are taken.

b Fruit naturally contains yeasts, so the fruit is sterilised. Sterile air is pumped into the drums to remove the fruit so that there is no risk of microorganisms contaminating it.

c Ultraviolet light destroys bacteria and fungal spores so keeping the area more hygienic.

4.4 An air lock at the entrance; laminar flow cabinet; smooth and easy-to-clean work surfaces, walls and floors; filtered air; designated 'clean zone'.

4.5 a The stirrer stirs contents of fermenter so that cells are constantly brought in contact with fresh medium.

b The water jacket contains cold water which circulates constantly to keep contents of fermenter from overheating.

c The acid/alkali inlet introduces acid or alkali as necessary to keep the pH constant.

d The sterile air inlet allows sterile air into the fermenter to provide oxygen for the cells if fermentation is aerobic. If the fermentation is anaerobic, carbon dioxide or nitrogen may be added, since a gas helps to mix the contents of the fermenter.

e The air outlet allows the waste gases and any sterile gas which has been introduced through the air inlet to escape from the fermenter.

4.6 The growth curve for continuous culture will resemble a normal batch culture curve except that, once the culture enters the logarithmic/exponential growth phase, the cell numbers are kept constant by removing cells and products and adding fresh nutrients at a carefully controlled rate (see figure).

● *Answer for* SAQ 4.6

The number of microorganisms present is kept constant because microorganisms are removed from the fermenter at the same rate as they are formed.

4.7 a To ensure purity of the source organism and to ensure antibiotic is being produced.

b Temperature, pH, oxygen levels, nutrients.

c *Temperature*: temperature probe plus cold water jacket to cool the fermenter.
pH: pH probe, pH adjusted by addition of buffer, acid or alkali.
Oxygen content: measured by oxygen probe. This would lead to adjustment of oxygen flow rate and mechanical stirring.
Nutrients: sometimes additional nutrients are added during the fermentation.

d The fermenter and medium would probably be steam sterilised. Chemical sterilisation of the fermenter may be carried out, but only in unusual circumstances.

e If some of the microorganisms have mutated, this would lead to the mutant organism being cultured and a changed product might result.

f *Advantages*: increases profit, reduces waste, low levels of antibiotic present control infections in animals.
Disadvantages: If animals are constantly exposed to low levels of antibiotics, their gut microorganisms develop antibiotic resistance, which can then be passed on to more harmful microorganisms like *Salmonella*. This means that the animals may develop infections which do not respond to antibiotics.

Chapter 5

5.1 Many possible answers could be given, including the ability to fix nitrogen, grow in saline soils, or produce increased yields.

5.2 Plant cells, even under optimum conditions, only divide slowly, perhaps once every 24 hours. Microbial cells, on the other hand, multiply rapidly. Therefore, if just one fungal spore or bacterial cell were to contaminate the plant tissue being cultured, the microorganism could outgrow the plant cells in just a few days.

5.3 People are concerned that the organisms might cause diseases or release toxins in humans or animals who accidentally ingest them. They are also concerned that they might mutate and become harmful; that they might compete with naturally present organisms, and that a bacterial insecticide might kill beneficial insects.

5.4 *Advantages*: increased milk yield per cow, therefore reducing costs by allowing the farmer to maintain a smaller herd. It can also help to overcome the seasonal shortfall of milk in August.
Disadvantages: Prolonged use of BST may weaken cows by depleting the immune system; in the EU there is already a milk surplus; cows need to eat more food when

given BST, and this cost can offset the additional milk yield; concern about consumers drinking milk or eating milk containing BST, particularly pregnant or nursing mothers.

5.5 This is to ensure that the strain of bacteria is kept pure, and that contaminating microorganisms which might produce other, harmful, substances do not multiply.

5.6 This is mainly because it keeps costs down. There is little point in using an existing food material since the cost of the single cell protein grown on such a substrate would be much more expensive. People will only use single cell protein as a food source if it is cheaper than existing foodstuffs. Waste products can be expensive for a company to dispose of, but if they can be used to make a saleable product this can make a profit instead.

5.7 They have rapid growth rates; they can utilise most waste substrates; there are no ethical problems; they can grow in fermenters which use a comparatively small land area; the fermenters are independent of climatic influences.

5.8 Because the actual product is the microorganism, it is more efficient to keep the organism in its exponential growth phase.

5.9 Milk may become contaminated with antibiotics if a cow has been treated with antibiotics, for example to treat mastitis, and the correct time has not elapsed before using her milk for human consumption. The milk used to make yogurt must be free from antibiotics, since antibiotics would destroy the bacteria used in the starter culture.

5.10 If the milk mixture is too hot, the bacteria in the starter culture will be destroyed.

5.11 This is because the bacteria produce acids, such as lactic acid and methanoic acid.

5.12 The bacteria are not harmful. Indeed, many people feel that 'live' yogurt is healthier and tastes better.

5.13 This sterilisation is necessary to ensure that contaminating microorganisms, such as yeasts, do not enter the yogurt, vats or pipework. This is usually done by steam sterilisation, although chemicals might be used if laboratory tests suggested that contamination had occurred.

5.14 The yeasts present on the skins of the fruit might be of different types, and some wine-makers wish to ensure uniformity by always using the same strain of yeast to make the wine.

5.15 The skins would be removed after a few days, so that they do not colour the wine as much as in a red wine.

5.16 Many wines undergo a spontaneous secondary fermentation during the second year, the malo-lactic fermentation, which converts malic acid to lactic acid and reduces the acidity of the wine.

5.17 A 'top-fermenting' yeast forms a thick frothy layer on top of the beer, whereas a 'bottom-fermenting' yeast forms a layer at the bottom of the fermenter. 'Top-fermenters' are mainly used for beer, while 'bottom-fermenters' are mainly used for lagers.

5.18 This is because the microorganisms are kept in their exponential growth phase in continuous fermenters. For organisms to be growing exponentially, conditions must be at their optimum, which means that waste products must be kept at lower levels. Alcohol is the waste product of the yeast, and if it accumulates, yeast growth slows down.

5.19 Breadmakers are interested in the carbon dioxide production of the yeast, whereas brewers are interested in alcohol production, so they select different strains.

5.20 Arguments for: improving palatability of meat; reducing the time needed in cold storage after slaughter, thereby saving costs and giving the meat a longer shelf-life. Main argument against: injection is distressing to the animal and may cause suffering.

Chapter 6

6.1   The biosensor would contain the enzyme glucose oxidase immobilised on the surface of the probe. In the presence of glucose in the blood, the enzyme would produce gluconic acid. This would generate a positive charge on the surface of the probe, causing a flow of electrons to the transducer, proportional to the glucose concentration in the blood. The current can be used to operate a pump which releases insulin into the bloodstream, and lowers the blood glucose level. The reduced blood glucose level would result in a lower current being received by the transducer, so the pump would slow down.

6.2   The probe of the biosensor could have an enzyme immobilised on its surface which breaks down cholesterol or alcohol to organic acids. The resulting drop in pH level would be detected by the transducer as a flow of electrons, and this current could be read on a meter. The current would be proportional to the amount of cholesterol or alcohol in the blood.

Chapter 7

7.1   A variety of other enzymes would have been present, including lipases and amylases.

7.2   The substrates mentioned are mainly carbohydrate-based. Whey contains a watery solution of lactose, molasses contains sucrose and starch, and flour waste is mainly starch.

7.3   Any suitable suggestion is acceptable, provided it is cheap, plentiful and non-toxic. One example might be water which has been used to wash potato slices prior to frozen chip or potato crisp manufacture.

7.4   Biological stains include food stains, such as egg or margarine, and stains from body fluids, such as blood or sweat.

7.5   The fermenter should include a container for the substrate to be placed inside: this might be a pit in the ground or some kind of storage vessel. It should incorporate a cover and a pipe for drawing off the biogas. Some provision would need to be made for adding more waste from time to time. The fermenter would need to be out-of-doors and not too close to houses for safety reasons as methane can be explosive.

7.6   This residue can be used as fertiliser.

Index (Numbers in italics refer to figures.)